# Collins

# AQA GCSE 9-1
# Maths
## Higher

Leisa Bovey

# Acknowledgements

The authors and publisher are grateful to the copyright holders for permission to use quoted materials and images.

Every effort has been made to trace copyright holders and obtain their permission for the use of copyright material. The authors and publisher will gladly receive information enabling them to rectify any error or omission in subsequent editions. All facts are correct at time of going to press.

All images ©Shutterstock and HarperCollins*Publishers*

Published by Collins
An imprint of HarperCollins*Publishers* Limited
1 London Bridge Street
London SE1 9GF

HarperCollins*Publishers*
Macken House
39/40 Mayor Street Upper
Dublin 1
D01 C9W8
Ireland

© HarperCollins*Publishers* Limited 2024

ISBN 978-0-00-867238-6

First published 2024

10 9 8 7 6 5 4 3 2 1

British Library Cataloguing in Publication Data.

A CIP record of this book is available from the British Library.

Author: Leisa Bovey
Publisher: Clare Souza
Commissioning and Project Management: Richard Toms
Editorial: Richard Toms, Anne Stothers and
Laura Connell (Maven Publishing)
Inside Concept Design: Ian Wrigley
Layout: Jouve Private India Limited and Nicola Lancashire
(Rose and Thorn Creative Services Limited)
Cover Design: Sarah Duxbury
Production: Bethany Brohm

Printed in India by Multivista Global Pvt.Ltd.

**MIX**
Paper | Supporting
responsible forestry
FSC™ C007454

This book contains FSC™ certified paper and other controlled sources to ensure responsible forest management.

For more information visit: www.harpercollins.co.uk/green

# How to use this book

Each topic is presented
on a two-page spread

Organise your
knowledge
with concise
explanations
and examples

**Key points**
highlight
fundamental
ideas

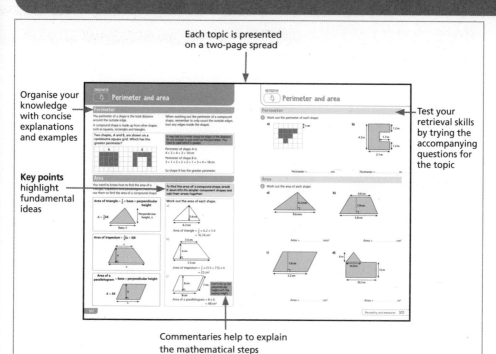

Test your
retrieval skills
by trying the
accompanying
questions for
the topic

Commentaries help to explain
the mathematical steps

**Mixed questions** further test
retrieval skills after all topics
have been covered

**Key facts and vocabulary**
section helps to consolidate
knowledge of mathematical
terms and concepts

**Answers** are provided to all
questions at the back of
the book

# Contents

# Contents

# (1) Written calculations

## Addition and subtraction

To add and subtract **integers**, line up the digits by place value and add or subtract each of them, starting with the ones.

When adding, you may need to carry to the next column on the left. When subtracting, you may need to exchange from the next column on the left.

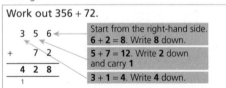

Work out 356 + 72.

Start from the right-hand side.
**6 + 2 = 8.** Write **8** down.
**5 + 7 = 12.** Write **2** down and carry **1**
**3 + 1 = 4.** Write **4** down.

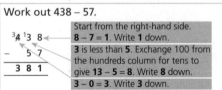

Work out 438 − 57.

Start from the right-hand side.
**8 − 7 = 1.** Write **1** down.
**3** is less than **5**. Exchange 100 from the hundreds column for tens to give **13 − 5 = 8**. Write **8** down.
**3 − 0 = 3.** Write **3** down.

## Multiplication

**Column multiplication:**
1. Write the number with the highest place value on top and line up the digits by place value.
2. Working from right to left, multiply the ones of the bottom number by each digit of the top number. If the product is more than 10, carry the tens digit.
3. Repeat for the tens of the bottom number. Do the same for all the digits of the bottom number.
4. Add up the results of each multiplication.

**Grid method:**
1. Partition the numbers into their place values. Write one partitioned number on top of the grid and the other to the side.
2. Multiply each part.
3. Add up the numbers inside the grid.

> For column multiplication, don't forget to include a zero in each row of the addition to show multiplication by tens, hundreds, etc. This is sometimes called a place holder.

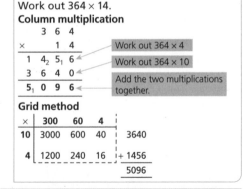

Work out 364 × 14.
**Column multiplication**

```
      3 6 4
×       1 4
  1  4₂5₁6          Work out 364 × 4
  3  6 4 0          Work out 364 × 10
  5₁0 9 6           Add the two multiplications
                    together.
```

**Grid method**

| ×  | 300  | 60  | 4  |        |
|----|------|-----|----|--------|
| 10 | 3000 | 600 | 40 | 3640   |
| 4  | 1200 | 240 | 16 | + 1456 |
|    |      |     |    | 5096   |

## Division

Write the number being divided (the **dividend**) inside the box and the number you are dividing by (the **divisor**) outside the box. The answer (the **quotient**) goes on top of the box. Divide each place value of the dividend by the divisor, starting with the largest place value.

**Short division:**
1. Divide each place value of the dividend by the divisor, starting with the largest place value.
2. If the divisor does not go into the dividend, write a zero above that place value. Write the remainder next to the next digit, carrying over.
3. Keep dividing until you have divided every place value of the dividend.

```
        0 1 3 8
1 2 | 2 1 ¹6 ⁴5 ⁹6
```

**Long division:**

Long division is similar to short division. It just involves showing your working to find the remainder at each place value rather than carrying it over at each step.

1. Divide
2. Multiply
3. Subtract
4. Bring down

```
            0 1 3 8
    1 2 | 2 1 6 5 6
        −   1 2
            ----
              4 5
            − 3 6
              ----
                9 6
```

# Written calculations

## Addition and subtraction

**1** Work out the following.

**a)**
```
  3 1 2
+ 4 6 9
```

**b)** 1782 + 53

**c)**
```
  9 3 6
- 8 5 4
```

**d)** 1284 – 38

## Multiplication

**2** Work out the following using your preferred method.

**a)**
```
  3 8 5
×   4 2
```

**b)** 89 × 14

**c)**
```
  2 5 3
×   3 7
```

**d)** 47 × 39

## Division

**3** Work out the following. Use either long or short division.

**a)** 7 $\overline{)5\ 7\ 4}$

**b)** 3396 ÷ 12

**c)** 16 $\overline{)8\ 4\ 8}$

**d)** 3969 ÷ 18

# 1 Fractions

## Adding and subtracting fractions

To add or subtract fractions, you must have a common **denominator**. Then add or subtract the **numerators**.

> Before adding or subtracting fractions, the denominators must be the same.

Work out $2\frac{2}{3} + 1\frac{1}{2}$

$2\frac{2}{3} + 1\frac{1}{2} = 2 + 1 + \frac{2}{3} + \frac{1}{2}$

$= 3 + \frac{4}{6} + \frac{3}{6}$ ← $\frac{2}{3} = \frac{4}{6}$ and $\frac{1}{2} = \frac{3}{6}$

$= 3 + 1\frac{1}{6}$ ← $\frac{4}{6} + \frac{3}{6} = \frac{7}{6} = 1\frac{1}{6}$

$= 4\frac{1}{6}$

Work out $4\frac{1}{4} - 2\frac{1}{2}$

**Method 1: Partition**

$4\frac{1}{4} - 2\frac{1}{2} = 4 - 2 + \frac{1}{4} - \frac{1}{2}$ ← Remember to subtract both the fraction and the whole number from the second term.

$= 2 - \frac{1}{4} = 1\frac{3}{4}$

**Method 2: Convert to improper fractions**

$4\frac{1}{4} - 2\frac{1}{2} = 4\frac{1}{4} - 2\frac{2}{4}$

$= \frac{17}{4} - \frac{10}{4}$ ← $4\frac{1}{4} = \frac{(4 \times 4) + 1}{4} = \frac{17}{4}$

$= \frac{7}{4} = 1\frac{3}{4}$ and $2\frac{2}{4} = \frac{(4 \times 2) + 2}{4} = \frac{10}{4}$

## Multiplying and dividing fractions

**To multiply fractions:**
1. Change any mixed numbers to improper fractions.
2. Multiply the numerators together.
3. Multiply the denominators together.
4. Simplify the answer if possible.

**To divide fractions:**
1. Convert any mixed numbers to improper fractions.
2. Remember KFC:
   **K**eep the first fraction as it is
   **F**lip the second fraction
   **C**hange ÷ to ×

> Remember to flip the second fraction when dividing fractions.

a) Work out $\frac{3}{4} \times \frac{3}{5}$

$\frac{3}{4} \times \frac{3}{5}$

$= \frac{9}{20}$

Simplify by dividing by 3.

b) Work out $2\frac{2}{3} \times 1\frac{1}{5}$

$2\frac{2}{3} \times 1\frac{1}{5} = \frac{8}{3} \times \frac{6}{5}$

$= \frac{8}{3^1} \times \frac{6^2}{5}$

$= \frac{16}{5}$

$= 3\frac{1}{5}$

a) Work out $\frac{5}{6} \div \frac{3}{5}$

$\frac{5}{6} \div \frac{3}{5} = \frac{5}{6} \times \frac{5}{3}$

$= \frac{25}{18}$

$= 1\frac{7}{18}$

b) Work out $1\frac{1}{4} \div 2\frac{1}{3}$

$1\frac{1}{4} \div 2\frac{1}{3} = \frac{5}{4} \div \frac{7}{3}$

$= \frac{5}{4} \times \frac{3}{7}$

$= \frac{15}{28}$

## Fractions of amounts

To work out a fraction of an amount, multiply the fraction by the amount.

$\frac{3}{4}$ of the 28 students in a class are boys. How many are girls?

You can either work out $\frac{1}{4}$ of 28 for the number of girls or $\frac{3}{4}$ of 28 for the number of boys and then subtract this from the total number of students.

$\frac{3}{4}$ of $28 = \frac{3}{4} \times 28 = \frac{3}{4^1} \times \frac{28^7}{1} = 21$

There are 21 boys, so there are: $28 - 21 = 7$ girls

**To write one quantity as a fraction of another:**
1. Write the amounts using the same units.
2. Write the fraction. The numerator is the amount and the denominator is the 'out of' number.

Write 30 cm as a fraction of 1 metre.

1 metre = 100 cm ← Make the units the same.

So 30 cm as a fraction of 1 metre is $\frac{30 \text{cm}}{100 \text{cm}} = \frac{3}{10}$

## 1 Fractions

## Adding and subtracting fractions

**1** Without a calculator, work out:

a) $3\frac{1}{3} + 4\frac{3}{4}$

b) $2\frac{3}{8} + 1\frac{1}{2}$

c) $3\frac{1}{2} - 2\frac{1}{3}$

d) $5\frac{2}{3} - 3\frac{1}{8}$

## Multiplying and dividing fractions

**2** Without a calculator, work out:

a) $2\frac{1}{3} \times 3\frac{3}{4}$

b) $1\frac{3}{8} \times 2\frac{1}{4}$

**3** Without a calculator, work out:

a) $2\frac{2}{5} \div 1\frac{1}{8}$

b) $3\frac{3}{4} \div \frac{2}{3}$

## Fractions of amounts

**4** a) Write 15 cm as a fraction of 1 m.

b) Write 30 mg as a fraction of 15 g.

**5** $\frac{3}{5}$ of a class of 30 students buy school dinners. The rest take a packed lunch.

How many students take a packed lunch?

# 1 Decimals

## Place value

This place value table shows the number 1234.567

The digit 5 has a value of 5 tenths or $\frac{5}{10}$

| Thousands | Hundreds | Tens | Ones | . | tenths | hundredths | thousandths |
|---|---|---|---|---|---|---|---|
| 1 | 2 | 3 | 4 | . | 5 | 6 | 7 |

| Write these numbers in ascending order: 2.33, 23.03, 3.022, 32.02, 2.303 | |
|---|---|
| 2.330, 23.030, 3.022, 32.020, 2.303 | Rewrite the numbers to the same number of decimal places. |
| 2.303, 2.33, 3.022, 23.03, 32.02 | Compare and order from lowest to highest by place value. Then write each number to the original number of decimal places. |

## Adding, subtracting, multiplying and dividing decimals

**To add and subtract decimals:**
1. Rewrite the numbers so that they have the same number of decimal places.
2. Line up the decimal points.
3. Add or subtract as usual.

Work out: a) 5.83 + 2.6    b) 3.4 − 1.28

a)
|   | 5 | . | 8 | 3 |
|---|---|---|---|---|
| + | 2 | . | 6 | 0 |
|   | 8 | . | 4 | 3 |
|   |   |   | 1 |   |

b)
|   | 3 | . | ³4 | ¹0 |
|---|---|---|---|---|
| − | 1 | . | 2 | 8 |
|   | 2 | . | 1 | 2 |

**To multiply decimals:**
1. Multiply the numbers as if the decimal point were not there.
2. Count how many decimal places are in the two numbers.
3. Put the decimal point into the product so that the number of decimal places is the same as the total in the two numbers being multiplied.

Work out 2.34 × 5.1

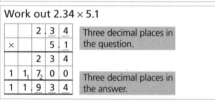

Three decimal places in the question.

Three decimal places in the answer.

**To divide a decimal by an integer:**
1. Bring up the decimal point into the answer.
2. Divide.

**To divide by a decimal:**
1. Count the number of decimal places in the divisor (the 'divided by' number).
2. Multiply both numbers by the power of 10 that will remove the decimal point.
3. Divide.

Work out:    Short division is used in these examples.

a)   13.2 ÷ 6

Line up the decimal points.

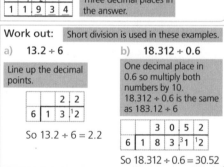

So 13.2 ÷ 6 = 2.2

b)   18.312 ÷ 0.6

One decimal place in 0.6 so multiply both numbers by 10.
18.312 ÷ 0.6 is the same as 183.12 ÷ 6

|   |   | 3 | 0 | 5 | 2 |
|---|---|---|---|---|---|
| 6 | 1 | 8 | 3 | ³1 | ¹2 |

So 18.312 ÷ 0.6 = 30.52

## Converting between decimals and fractions

| Express 0.24 as a fraction in its simplest form. | |
|---|---|
| $0.24 = \frac{24}{100} = \frac{6}{25}$ | The smallest place value is hundredths, so use 100 as the denominator. |

Write 0.1̇2̇ as a fraction.

$x = 0.\dot{1}\dot{2}$

$100x = 12.\dot{1}\dot{2}$    Multiply by 100 to shift the digits by two places.

$99x = 12$    Subtract the original equation.

$x = \frac{12}{99}$

So $0.\dot{1}\dot{2} = \frac{12}{99} = \frac{4}{33}$

Express as decimals:    Add a decimal point to the divisor and bring it up to the answer.

a) $\frac{3}{8}$

|   | 0 | . | 3 | 7 | 5 |
|---|---|---|---|---|---|
| 8 | 3 | . | 0 | ⁶0 | ⁴0 |

$\frac{3}{8} = 0.375$

b) $\frac{2}{3}$

|   | 0 | . | 6 | 6 | 6... |
|---|---|---|---|---|---|
| 3 | 2 | . | 0 | ²0 | ²0 |

$\frac{2}{3} = 0.666...$

If you see the same digit (or sequence of digits) repeating in the answer, it is a recurring decimal.

#  Decimals

## Place value

1 Order these numbers from least to greatest:

0.805        8.05        0.85        0.588        8.5

## Adding, subtracting, multiplying and dividing decimals

2 Without a calculator, work out:

**a)** $17.99 + 2.3$

**b)** $54.9 - 1.62$

3 Without a calculator, work out:

**a)** $7.6 \times 6.2$

**b)** $10.33 \times 3.7$

4 Without a calculator, work out:

**a)** $42.6 \div 6$

**b)** $67.2 \div 0.7$

## Converting between decimals and fractions

5 Express:

**a)** 0.512 as a fraction in its simplest form

**b)** $\frac{5}{8}$ as a decimal.

# Multiples, factors and primes

## Multiples and lowest common multiple

**Multiples** are the numbers in the times table of a given number. The **lowest common multiple** (**LCM**) of two or more integers is the smallest of the multiples in common.

> Numbers can have many common multiples, but only one *lowest* common multiple.

> Work out the LCM of 3 and 4.
>
> Multiples of 3: 3  6  9  (12)  15  18  21  (24) ...
>
> Multiples of 4: 4  8  (12)  16  20  (24)  30  36 ...
>
> 12 and 24 are in both lists; they are common multiples of 3 and 4.
>
> The LCM of 3 and 4 is 12.

## Factors and highest common factor

**Factors** are numbers that divide evenly into another number without a remainder.

When two or more integers have factors that are the same, these are called **common factors**. The highest of these is the **highest common factor (HCF)**.

> Work out the HCF of 12 and 18.
>
> The factors of 12 are    1  (2)(3)  4  (6)  12
>
> The factors of 18 are    1  (2)(3)(6)  9  18
>
> 2, 3 and 6 are all common factors of 12 and 18.
>
> So 6 is the highest common factor of 12 and 18.

## Prime factorisation

A **prime number** is a number whose only factors are one and itself. A **composite number** is a number that is not prime.

Any integer can be written as a product of prime numbers.

> Try to memorise the prime numbers up to 100:
> 2, 3, 5, 7, 11, 13, 17, 19, 23, 29, 31, 37, 41, 43, 47, 53, 59, 61, 67, 71, 73, 79, 83, 89, 97

> Write 24 as a product of prime factors.
>
> ```
>        24
>       /   \
>      4  ×  6
>    /  \   /  \
>  2 × 2  2 × 3
> ```
>
> Pick two numbers that when multiplied together give 24.
>
> Repeat for 4 and 6.
>
> Stop when you reach a prime number.
>
> So $24 = 2 \times 2 \times 2 \times 3$ — This is called a product of prime factors.
>
> $= 2^3 \times 3$ — Product of prime factors in **index form**.

## Using prime factors to work out the HCF and LCM

**To work out the HCF and LCM using prime factors:**

1. Find the prime factors of both numbers.
2. The HCF is the product of the common prime factors.
3. The LCM is the product of the HCF and the remaining factors.

> The LCM of two numbers is 24.
> The HCF of the same two numbers is 4.
> Work out the two numbers.
>
> Factors of 24 are    1, 2, 3, 4, 6, 8, 12, 24
>
> Numbers that are also multiples of 4 are
>
> 4, 8, 12, 24
>
> Now find pairs where the LCM is 24 and the HCF is 4.
>
> There are two possible answers:
>
> 8 and 12 or 4 and 24

You can use a Venn diagram to work out the HCF and LCM of a pair of numbers in a visual way.

> Work out the HCF and LCM of 24 and 60.
>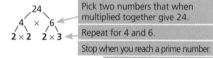
> $24 = (2) \times (2) \times 2 \times (3)$
> $60 = (2) \times (2) \times (3) \times 5$
>
>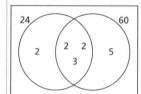
>
> Draw factor trees for both numbers. Each product has two 2s and one 3.
>
> The HCF is $2 \times 2 \times 3 = 12$
> The LCM is $12 \times 2 \times 5 = 120$

#  Multiples, factors and primes

## Multiples and lowest common multiple

1 Work out the lowest common multiple of:

**a)**  12 and 30

**b)**  5 and 15

## Factors and highest common factor

2 Work out the highest common factor of:

**a)**  16 and 72

**b)**  8 and 20

## Prime factorisation

3 Write these numbers as products of primes.

**a)**  32

**b)**  40

## Using prime factors to work out the HCF and LCM

4 Use prime factors to work out:

**a)**  the HCF of 32 and 40

**b)**  the LCM of 32 and 40

# (1) Powers and roots

## Indices

A **power**, or **index** (plural: indices), is a short way of writing a number multiplied by itself. The power is the number of times the number is multiplied by itself. The number being multiplied is called the **base**.

$$8^5 = 8 \times 8 \times 8 \times 8 \times 8$$

Base Power (or index)

In words, this is said '8 to the power of 5'.

> You should memorise all the squared numbers up to $15^2$ and all the cube numbers up to $5^3$.

## Using the laws of indices

Make sure you know the laws of indices:

| To multiply indices of the same base, add the powers | $3^4 \times 3^5 = 3^{(4+5)} = 3^9$ |
|---|---|
| To divide indices of the same base, subtract the powers | $6^7 \div 6^2 = 6^{(7-2)} = 6^5$ |
| To raise a power of a number to another power, multiply the powers | $(4^3)^5 = 4^{3 \times 5} = 4^{15}$ |
| A number raised to a negative power is the **reciprocal** of the positive power | $8^{(-4)} = \frac{1}{8^4}$ |
| Any number to the power of 1 is itself | $7^1 = 7$ |
| Any number to the power of 0 is 1 | $326^0 = 1$ |

> Make sure you know how to find powers and roots on your calculator.

The laws of indices also work with variables.

For example:

$x^3 \times x^4 = x^7$

$y^{\frac{1}{3}} = \sqrt[3]{y}$

$\frac{k^4 \times k^5}{k^3} = \frac{k^{(4+5)}}{k^3} = \frac{k^9}{k^3}$

$\frac{k^9}{k^3} = k^{(9-3)} = k^6$

a) Write $6^4 \times 6^5$ as a single power of 6.

$6^4 \times 6^5 = 6^{(4+5)} = 6^9$

b) Write $5^8 \div 5^4$ as a single power of 5.

$5^8 \div 5^4 = 5^{(8-4)} = 5^4$

c) Simplify $\frac{4^6 \times 4^2}{4^5}$    $\frac{4^6 \times 4^2}{4^5} = \frac{4^8}{4^5} = 4^3$

d) Simplify $\frac{3^8 \times 3^3}{3^7}$    $\frac{3^8 \times 3^3}{3^7} = \frac{3^{11}}{3^7} = 3^4$

## Roots and fractional powers

The **root** of a given number is the number that when multiplied by itself results in the given number.

The **square root** of a given number is the number that is squared to result in the given number.

The **cube root** of a given number is the number that is cubed to result in the given number.

For example:

$\sqrt[3]{64} = 4$ because $4^3 = 64$

$\sqrt[5]{243} = 3$ because $3^5 = 243$

A **fractional power** is another way of writing a root.

$16^{\frac{1}{4}} = \sqrt[4]{16} = 2$ because $2^4 = 16$

When the numerator of the fraction is not 1, that means the root is being raised to a power. You can also have negative fractional powers.

a) Work out $8^{\frac{2}{3}}$

$8^{\frac{2}{3}} = \left(8^{\frac{1}{3}}\right)^2$    ← $\frac{2}{3} = \frac{1}{3} \times 2$ so rewrite as $8^{\frac{1}{3}}$ squared.

$= \left(\sqrt[3]{8}\right)^2$    ← $8^{\frac{1}{3}} = \sqrt[3]{8}$

$= 2^2 = 4$    ← It's always easier to work out the root first.

b) Work out $64^{-\frac{2}{3}}$

$64^{-\frac{2}{3}} = \frac{1}{64^{\frac{2}{3}}} = \frac{1}{(\sqrt[3]{64})^2} = \frac{1}{4^2} = \frac{1}{16}$

> A negative power means the reciprocal of the positive power.

**Powers and roots**

## Indices

1 Work out the value of:

   **a)** $2^6$                 **b)** $5^4$                 **c)** $18^3$

## Using the laws of indices

2 Simplify:

   **a)** $3^4 \times 3^7$

   **b)** $7^5 \div 7^2$

   **c)** $\dfrac{x^2 \times x^6}{x^3}$

## Roots and fractional powers

3 Work out the value of:

   **a)** $16^{\frac{3}{4}}$

   **b)** $125^{\frac{2}{3}}$

   **c)** $25^{-\frac{3}{2}}$

# 1 Surds

## Rational numbers

A **rational number** can be written as a fraction $\frac{a}{b}$ where both $a$ and $b$ are integers.

If a number cannot be written as a fraction, it is an **irrational number**.

Integers, fractions, terminating decimals and recurring decimals are all rational numbers.

> Remember that recurring decimals can be written as fractions.

| Examples of rational numbers | Examples of irrational numbers |
|---|---|
| $2.3 = \frac{23}{10}$ $0.\dot{6} = \frac{2}{3}$ $12 = \frac{12}{1}$ | $\pi$ $\sqrt{2}$ |

## Simplifying and calculating with surds

A **surd** is a root that cannot be simplified to a rational number. A surd is an **exact answer**. At GCSE, you will only work with surds involving squares.

**Rules for simplifying and calculating with surds**

$$\sqrt{a \times b} = \sqrt{a} \times \sqrt{b}$$

$$\sqrt{a} \times \sqrt{a} = a$$

$$\sqrt{\frac{a}{b}} = \frac{\sqrt{a}}{\sqrt{b}} \text{ (or } \sqrt{a} \div \sqrt{b})$$

When adding and subtracting surds, the number inside the surd must be the same.

For example, $\sqrt{a} + \sqrt{a} = 2\sqrt{a}$

You cannot add or subtract surds of different numbers.

Expanding brackets with surds is just like expanding brackets with variables (see page 22).

a) Simplify $\sqrt{5} \times \sqrt{20}$

$\sqrt{5} \times \sqrt{20} = \sqrt{5 \times 20}$

$\qquad = \sqrt{100}$

$\qquad = 10$

b) Write the value of $\sqrt{\frac{5}{16}}$

$\sqrt{\frac{5}{16}} = \frac{\sqrt{5}}{\sqrt{16}}$

$\qquad = \frac{\sqrt{5}}{4}$

c) Expand $(2 + \sqrt{3})(5 - \sqrt{3})$

| | 2 | $\sqrt{3}$ |
|---|---|---|
| 5 | 10 | $5\sqrt{3}$ |
| $-\sqrt{3}$ | $-2\sqrt{3}$ | $-3$ |

$-\sqrt{3} \times \sqrt{3} = -\sqrt{9} = -3$

$= 10 + 5\sqrt{3} - 2\sqrt{3} - 3$

$= 7 + 3\sqrt{3}$ ◄── Simplify.

> Surds can be simplified if the number under the square root surd has a square number as a factor.

Simplify $\sqrt{75}$

$\sqrt{75} = \sqrt{25 \times 3}$ ◄── The largest square factor of 75 is 25.

$\qquad = \sqrt{25} \times \sqrt{3} = 5 \times \sqrt{3}$

$\qquad = 5\sqrt{3}$ ◄── Simplify.

## Rationalising the denominator

If a fraction has a surd as the denominator, you can use the concept of equivalent fractions to turn the denominator into a rational number by multiplying the numerator and the denominator by the surd.

Rationalise the denominator and simplify $\frac{10}{\sqrt{5}}$

$\frac{10}{\sqrt{5}} = \frac{10}{\sqrt{5}} \times \frac{\sqrt{5}}{\sqrt{5}}$

$\qquad = \frac{10\sqrt{5}}{5}$ ◄── Cancel the 10 and the 5.

$\qquad = 2\sqrt{5}$

If the denominator includes a surd added or subtracted to a rational number, change the sign in the expression and multiply by that expression.

Rationalise the denominator of $\frac{3}{2 + \sqrt{7}}$ and simplify.

$\frac{3}{2 + \sqrt{7}} \times \frac{2 - \sqrt{7}}{2 - \sqrt{7}} = \frac{3(2 - \sqrt{7})}{(2 + \sqrt{7})(2 - \sqrt{7})}$

> Change the sign of $2 + \sqrt{7}$ and multiply by $2 - \sqrt{7}$.

$\qquad = \frac{6 - 3\sqrt{7}}{-3} = -2 + \sqrt{7}$

> Divide the numerator and denominator by $-3$.

# Surds

## Rational numbers

1 Which of the numbers in the box are rational? Show workings for your answers.

$2\sqrt{7}$    $\sqrt{16}$    $3$    $5.03$    $\sqrt{32}$

$0.\dot{4}$    $\sqrt{3}$

$\sqrt{12}$    $0.7\dot{5}\dot{3}$    $0.1283$

$\frac{2}{3}$    $\frac{8}{5}$

........................................................................................................................

........................................................................................................................

........................................................................................................................

........................................................................................................................

## Simplifying and calculating with surds

2 Simplify:

a) $\sqrt{72}$

b) $3 + \sqrt{5} - 2\sqrt{5}$

c) $3\sqrt{27} + 2\sqrt{3}$

## Rationalising the denominator

3 Rationalise the denominator of the following and simplify if possible.

a) $\frac{3}{\sqrt{10}}$

b) $\frac{4}{\sqrt{32}}$

c) $\frac{5}{2 + \sqrt{3}}$

# 1 Rounding and standard index form

## Rounding and significant figures

**To round to a given place value or a given number of decimal places (d.p.):**

1. Look at the place value (or decimal place) to the right of the given place value.
2. If the digit is greater than or equal to 5, round the digit up.
3. If the digit is less than 5, leave the digit unchanged.

To round to a certain number of **significant figures (s.f.)**, count the significant figures from left to right and round to that place value.

Round 231.6754 to 1 decimal place.

Look at the digit in the second decimal place.

231.6$\underline{7}$54

7 is greater than 5, so round to 231.7

231.6754 is closer to 231.7 than to 231.6

| H | T | O | | t | h | th | tth |
|---|---|---|---|---|---|----|-----|
| 2 | 3 | 1 | . | 6 | 7 | 5  | 4   |

A place value table can help you look at the correct digit.

---

Write 231.6754 to 1 significant figure.

②31.6754 ⟵ The first significant figure is 2.

②31.6754 ⟵ To round to 1 significant figure, round to the nearest hundreds.

②31.6754 ⟵ Look at the tens digit. 3 is less than 5, so round down.

231.6754 is 200 to 1 s.f.

The first significant figure is the first non-zero digit in the number. However, a zero is significant if it comes after the first significant figure.

Write 0.003 219 to 2 significant figures.

0.003②19 ⟵ The second significant figure is the digit 2 in the ten thousandths place.

0.003②19 ⟵ The digit to the right (1) is less than 5, so don't round up.

So 0.0032 to 2 s.f.

## Standard index form

A number in standard form is written as a power of 10. It has one digit to the left of the decimal point.

A number in standard form is written as $a \times 10^n$ where $a$ is $1 \le a < 10$ and $n$ is an integer. The value of $n$ tells you how many places the digits have moved.

Write in standard form:

a) **64 700**

$64\,700 = 6.47 \times 10^4$

Digits have moved four places.

b) **0.002**

$0.002 = 2 \times 10^{-3}$

Digits have moved three places.

For large numbers, $n$ is positive, e.g. 312 000 in standard form is $3.12 \times 10^5$

For small numbers (less than 1), $n$ is negative, e.g. 0.5709 in standard form is $5.709 \times 10^{-1}$

To calculate with numbers in standard form, first convert them to ordinary form, do the calculation, and then convert back to standard form.

Write each of these as an ordinary number.

a) $5 \times 10^3$     b) $4.8 \times 10^{-2}$

$5 \times 10^3 = 5000$     $4.8 \times 10^{-2} = 0.048$

## Limits of accuracy

Any measurement is performed to a given degree of accuracy. The actual measurement will lie between an **upper bound** and a **lower bound**.

The limits of accuracy are always plus and minus half of the degree of accuracy.

---

A carpenter measures a table as 123 cm by 209 cm to the nearest centimetre. Calculate the smallest possible area of the table, giving your answer in m².

Using inequality notation, the upper and lower bounds of the width, $w$, and length, $l$, are 122.5 cm $\le w <$ 123.5 cm and 208.5 cm $\le l <$ 209.5 cm.

The lower bound of the area is 1.225 m × 2.085 m = 2.55 m²

The measurements are given to 3 s.f. so give the answer to 3 s.f.

#  Rounding and standard index form

## Rounding and significant figures

1. Round:

   a) 805.997 to 2 decimal places

   b) 45 578.920 27 to the nearest hundredth

   c) 1243.304 to the nearest ten

2. Round:

   a) 1273.097 to 1 significant figure

   b) 107.896 to 2 significant figures

   c) 0.007 8064 to 3 significant figures

## Standard index form

3. Write in standard form:

   a) 13 400

   b) 906 000 000

   c) 0.032 38

4. Write as ordinary numbers:

   a) $1.306 \times 10^6$

   b) $9.81 \times 10^3$

   c) $2.87 \times 10^{-4}$

## Limits of accuracy

5. Work out the limits of accuracy and express them using inequality notation.

   a) The length of a football field measured as 98 m to the nearest metre.

   b) The length of an ant measured as 2 mm to the nearest millimetre.

6. 150 ml of olive oil (measured to the nearest millilitre) weighs 140 g (measured to the nearest gram). Work out the upper bound of the density of olive oil. Give your answer to 3 significant figures.

   $$\text{Density} = \frac{\text{Mass}}{\text{Volume}}$$

   _____ g/ml

# 2 Algebraic expressions

## Vocabulary

| Vocabulary | Meaning | Examples |
|---|---|---|
| Variable | A letter that is used to represent any number | $x$ or $n$ |
| Coefficient | A number that multiplies a variable | $3x$ or $2y$ |
| Constant | A number that does not have a variable attached to it | 4 or 8 |
| Term | One part of an expression, equation, formula or identity | $2x - 3y + 4$ has the three terms $2x$, $-3y$ and $+4$ |
| Expression | A combination of variables with numbers and operations | $2x + 3y$ or $\frac{x}{2} + 1$ |
| Equation | Contains an equals sign and at least one variable | $2x + 5 = 16$ or $x + 3y = 7$ |
| Formula | A rule connecting more than one variable; it also has an equals sign | $A = \pi r^2$ or $s = \frac{d}{t}$ |
| Identity | Contains an identity sign and is true for all values | $x + x \equiv 2x$ or $(x + 5)^2 \equiv x^2 + 10x + 25$ |
| Inequality | This is like an equation except that the two sides are **not** equal | $3x - 2 > x + 4$ |

## Simplifying expressions

**Like terms** are terms that have the same variable. To **simplify** an expression means to combine or collect like terms, e.g. $2x$ and $3x$ or $3k^2$ and $4k^2$. You should give answers in their simplest form.

Simplify:

a) $3x + 4x$

Collect like terms.

$3x + 4x = 7x$

b) $x^2 + 4x - 7x + 3x^2$

$x^2 + 4x - 7x + 3x^2$

$= 4x^2 - 3x$

$x^2 + 3x^2 = 4x^2$
$4x - 7x = -3x$

c) $xy + 3yx - 2xy$

$xy$ is the same as $yx$.

$xy + 3yx - 2xy = 2xy$

## Substitution

To **substitute** a number into an expression means to replace the given variable with the number.

If $x = 2$, $y = -3$ and $z = 0$, work out the value of:

a) $5x - 4y$

$5x - 4y = 5 \times 2 - 4 \times -3$ ← Substitute the values for $x$ and $y$.

$= 10 + 12$ ← Show your working out.

$= 22$

b) $xyz$

$xyz = 2 \times -3 \times 0$ ← Substitute the values for $x$, $y$ and $z$.

$= 0$

c) $y^2 - x$

$y^2 - x = (-3)^2 - 2$ ← Use brackets as the minus sign is also squared.

$= 9 - 2$ ← Show your working out.

$= 7$

## Writing expressions

To write an expression, start by writing what the variables represent. It can help to write out the expression in words and then replace the words with variables.

A rectangle has a width of $w$. Its length is 2 cm less than its width.

Write an expression for the perimeter of the rectangle.

$(w - 2)$ cm

$w$ cm

The perimeter is found by adding up all the sides:

$w + (w - 2) + w + (w - 2) = 4w - 4$

An expression for the perimeter is $(4w - 4)$ cm, where $w$ is the width of the rectangle.

## ② Algebraic expressions

## Vocabulary

**1** You are given that $s^2 + 3su - 4$

    **a)** Is this an identity, expression, equation or inequality? .............................................

    **b)** Complete the table.

|  | Terms | Variables | Coefficients | Constants |
|---|---|---|---|---|
| $s^2 + 3su - 4$ |  |  |  |  |

## Simplifying expressions

**2** Simplify each expression.

    **a)** $3x + 5y - 5x + 3$

.............................................

    **b)** $4j^2 + 3j - 1 + 2j - 4$

.............................................

    **c)** $5k - 7 + 3k - 9k + 1$

.............................................

## Substitution

**3** **a)** Work out the value of $x$ in $x = 2y + 4z - 1$, when $y = -4$ and $z = 5$.

$x = $ .............................................

    **b)** Work out the value of $R$ in $R = \frac{3x - 2t}{2}$, when $x = 2$ and $t = 1$.

$R = $ .............................................

## Writing expressions

**4** A t-shirt costs £15 and trousers cost £25.

Write an expression for the cost in pounds of buying $s$ t-shirts and $t$ trousers.

£ .............................................................................................................................

# (2) Expanding brackets

## One set of brackets

To **expand** or **multiply out** brackets means to multiply each term within the brackets using the **distributive law**.

The distributive law
$$a(b + c) = ab + ac$$
$$a(b - c) = ab - ac$$

Expand the brackets and simplify $3(2x - 4) + 2(x + 1)$.

Using a grid method to expand $3(2x - 4)$.

$3(2x - 4)$

| × | $2x$ | $-4$ |
|---|------|------|
| 3 | $6x$ | $-12$ |

$= 6x - 12$

$3 \times 2x = 6x$  $3 \times -4 = -12$

Using a grid method to expand $2(x + 1)$.

$2(x + 1)$

| × | $x$ | 1 |
|---|-----|---|
| 2 | $2x$ | 2 |

$= 2x + 2$

$2 \times x = 2x$  $2 \times 1 = 2$

Combine like terms.

$3(2x - 4) + 2(x + 1) = 6x - 12 + 2x + 2$

$= 8x - 10$

Make sure you multiply the term outside the bracket by every term inside the bracket, and keep track of any negative signs.

## Two sets of brackets

To multiply or expand two sets of brackets, you must multiply everything from the first by everything in the second. You can use a grid to help you. Alternatively, when both brackets have two terms you can use the acronym FOIL to help you keep track of the terms.

Multiply **every** term in the first bracket by **every** term in the second bracket.

| Grid method | FOIL method |
|---|---|
| 1. Partition the terms in both brackets. | **Firsts:** multiply the first terms. |
| 2. Write the terms from one bracket on the top of the grid. | **Outers:** multiply the outer terms. |
| 3. Write the terms of the other bracket to the side. | **Inners:** multiply the inner terms. |
| 4. Multiply each part and find the sum. | **Lasts:** multiply the last terms. |

Firsts — Lasts
$(a + b)(c + d)$
Outers  Inners

Multiply out $(2x + 3)(x - 1)$

**Grid method**

Partition each bracket and multiply each term.

| × | $2x$ | 3 |
|---|------|---|
| $x$ | $2x^2$ | $3x$ |
| $-1$ | $-2x$ | $-3$ |

$= 2x^2 + 3x - 2x - 3$

$= 2x^2 + x - 3$

**Using FOIL**

$(2x + 3)(x - 1) = (2x \times x) + (2x \times -1) + (3 \times x) + (3 \times -1)$
$= 2x^2 - 2x + 3x - 3$
$= 2x^2 + x - 3$

## Three sets of brackets

To expand more than two brackets, expand the first two then multiply by the third, and so on.

Multiply out $(y + 3)(y - 2)(y + 1)$.

Expand the first two brackets.

$(y + 3)(y - 2) = y^2 + y - 6$

Multiply the product by the third bracket.

$(y^2 + y - 6)(y + 1) = y^3 + 2y^2 - 5y - 6$

| × | $y^2$ | $y$ | $-6$ |
|---|-------|-----|------|
| $y$ | $y^3$ | $y^2$ | $-6y$ |
| 1 | $y^2$ | $y$ | $-6$ |

Simplify the terms inside the grid.
$y^2 + y^2 = 2y^2$
$-6y + y = -5y$

# ② Expanding brackets

## One set of brackets

**1** Expand and simplify $3(x - 3) - 2(x + 4)$

## Two sets of brackets

**2** Multiply out:

**a)** $(x - 3)(2x + 5)$

**b)** $(2x + 1)(3x - 5)$

**3** Expand and simplify $(3x - 1)(2x + 4) - 5x + 8$

## Three sets of brackets

**4** Multiply out $(m - 4)(m + 3)(2m + 1)$

# (2) Factorising expressions

## Factorising

To **factorise** means to write an expression as a multiplication, or to pull out a common factor.

> Find the HCF of the coefficients and variables.

Factorise $8xy - 6x^2$.

The HCF of $8xy$ and $-6x^2$ is $2x$.
$8xy = 2x \times 4y$ and $-6x^2 = 2x \times -3x$
Then, $8xy - 6x^2 = 2x(4y - 3x)$

| $\times$ | $4y$ | $-3x$ | |
|---|---|---|---|
| $2x$ | $8xy$ | $-6x^2$ | $= 2x(4y - 3x)$ |

⌐ HCF of $8xy$ and $-6x^2$

## Quadratic expressions of the form $x^2 + bx + c$

**Factorising using a grid:**
1. Write the $x^2$ term in the top left and the $c$ term in the bottom right.
2. Find two terms that multiply to $cx^2$ and add to $bx$. Write them in the empty spots in the grid.
3. Find the HCF of each row and column of the grid. Write the result in brackets.

**Factorising without a grid:**
1. Write two brackets with $x$ as the first term in both, $(x \quad )(x \quad )$.
2. If $c$ is negative, one number will be positive and the other negative.
3. Find two numbers that multiply to $c$ and add to $b$. Write those two numbers as the second term in the brackets.

Factorise $x^2 - x - 12$.
**Using a grid**

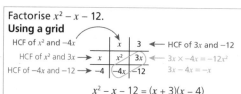

HCF of $x^2$ and $-4x$
HCF of $x^2$ and $3x$
HCF of $-4x$ and $-12$

HCF of $3x$ and $-12$
$3x \times -4x = -12x^2$
$3x - 4x = -x$

$$x^2 - x - 12 = (x + 3)(x - 4)$$

> $c$ is negative, so one number will be positive and one negative.

**Without a grid**
$x^2 - x - 12 = (x + \quad )(x - \quad )$
$= (x + 3)(x - 4)$

> Write $+3$ and $-4$ in the brackets.

$3x$ and $-4x$ sum to $-x$ and multiply to $-12x^2$.

## Quadratic expressions of the form $ax^2 + bx + c$

**Factorising using a grid:**
Follow the steps for factorising quadratics of the form $x^2 + bx + c$, except find two terms that multiply to $ax^2 \times c$ and sum to $bx$.

**Factorising without a grid:**
1. Find two terms that multiply to $ax^2 \times c$ and add to $bx$. Substitute those terms for $bx$.
2. Factorise the first two terms and the second two terms separately (i.e. factorise in parts).
3. Combine into two brackets.

Factorise $6x^2 + 7x - 3$.

**Using a grid**

$6x^2 \times -3 = -18x^2$ so find two terms that multiply to $-18x^2$ and sum to $7x$.
$9x \times (-2x) = -18x^2$ and $9x - 2x = 7x$

HCF of $6x^2$ and $2x$
HCF of $6x^2$ and $9x$
HCF of $-2x$ and $-3$

| | $2x$ | $3$ | |
|---|---|---|---|
| $3x$ | $6x^2$ | $9x$ | ← HCF of $9x$ and $-3$ |
| $-1$ | $-2x$ | $-3$ | |

$9x \times -2x = -18x^2$
$9x - 2x = 7x$

$$6x^2 + 7x - 3 = (3x - 1)(2x + 3)$$

**Without a grid**
$6x^2 + 7x - 3 = 6x^2 + 9x - 2x - 3$
$= 3x(2x + 3) - 1(2x + 3)$
$= (3x - 1)(2x + 3)$

> $9x$ and $-2x$ multiply to $-18x^2$ and add to $7x$.

> Factorise in parts. The terms in the brackets must be the same in both parts.

$6x^2 - 9x = 3x(2x + 3)$
and $-2x - 3 = -1(2x + 3)$

## Difference of two squares

A quadratic expression that is the difference of two squares (in the form $a^2 - b^2$) can be quickly factorised into $(a + b)(a - b)$. This rule also works when the coefficient is a square number.

Factorise $4x^2 - 9$.

> Recognise that $4x^2$ is a square number and so is $9$.

Using the difference of two squares $4x^2 - 9 = (2x + 3)(2x - 3)$

# ② Factorising expressions

## Factorising

**1** **a)** Factorise $3a + 9b$

**b)** Factorise $5x + 20xy$

## Quadratic expressions of the form $x^2 + bx + c$

**2** **a)** Factorise $x^2 - 3x - 4$

**b)** Factorise $k^2 + k - 6$

## Quadratic expressions of the form $ax^2 + bx + c$

**3** **a)** Factorise $2x^2 + 5x + 3$

**b)** Factorise $4m^2 - 4m - 3$

## Difference of two squares

**4** **a)** Factorise $25y^2 - 100$

**b)** Factorise $16b^2 - 81$

## Using and writing formulae

A **formula** is a rule that relates two or more variables.

The **subject** of a formula is what you are using the formula to find. It is on its own on one side of the equals sign.

To use a formula, substitute the known values in for the variables and calculate.

$A = l \times w$ relates the area ($A$) of a rectangle to its length ($l$) and width ($w$).

$$A = l \times w$$

Subject     Variables

To find the area, substitute in the length and width.

Follow the order of operations (BIDMAS) when substituting values.

Brackets

Indices

Division & Multiplication (left to right)

Addition & Subtraction (left to right)

A taxi firm charges a base rate of £5 and an additional £1.20 per mile travelled.

a) Write a formula for the taxi fare.

Cost = £5 + £1.20 × miles travelled

As a formula, $C = 5 + 1.2m$, where $m$ is the number of miles travelled and $C$ is the total cost in pounds.   *C is the subject.*

b) Work out the cost of an 8-mile journey.

$C = 5 + 1.2m$   ← Substitute $m = 8$

$C = 5 + (1.2 \times 8) = 5 + 9.6 = 14.6$

The fare is £14.60

c) Charlie's taxi fare was £23. Work out the distance she travelled.

$C = 5 + 1.2m$

$23 = 5 + 1.2m$   ← Substitute the known values.

$18 = 1.2m$   ← Subtract 5 from both sides.

$m = 18 \div 1.2 = 15$

The taxi travelled 15 miles.

Alternatively, you can rearrange the formula to solve for $m$ first.

## Rearranging a formula to change the subject

You will often need to find the value of a variable that is not the subject of the formula. To change the subject of a formula, use inverse operations to isolate the subject. You may also need to factorise or expand brackets.

a) Rearrange to make $x$ the subject of $y = 3x + 2$.

$y - 2 = 3x$   ← Subtract 2 from both sides.

$\frac{y-2}{3} = x$   ← Divide both sides by 3.

b) Rearrange to make $P$ the subject of $A = P + \frac{PRT}{100}$

$100A = 100P + PRT$   ← Multiply each term by 100 to remove the fraction.

$100A = P(100 + RT)$   ← Factorise $P$ (the subject).

$P = \frac{100A}{100 + RT}$

Divide both sides by $100 + RT$ to isolate $P$.

c) Rearrange the formula $J = 5\pi \sqrt{\frac{3K}{N}}$ to make $K$ the subject.

$J = 5\pi \sqrt{\frac{3K}{N}}$

$\frac{J}{5\pi} = \sqrt{\frac{3K}{N}}$   ← Divide both sides by $5\pi$.

$\left(\frac{J}{5\pi}\right)^2 = \frac{3K}{N}$   ← Square both sides to remove the square root.

$\frac{J^2}{25\pi^2} \times N = 3K$   ← Multiply both sides by $N$ to get $N$ out of the denominator.

$K = \frac{NJ^2}{25\pi^2} \div 3$   ← Divide both sides by 3 to isolate $K$.

$K = \frac{NJ^2}{25\pi^2} \times \frac{1}{3}$   ← Remember 'Keep, Flip, Change' ('KFC') to divide with fractions.

$K = \frac{NJ^2}{75\pi^2}$

## 2 Formulae

## Using and writing formulae

**1** A plumber charges a call-out fee of £130 plus an hourly rate of £65.

   **a)** Write a formula for the amount the plumber charges in total.

.....................................................................................................................................................

   **b)** How much does the plumber charge for a 4-hour job?

£ .........................................

**2** The value of money in an account with compound interest can be found using the formula

$T = P\left(1 + \frac{r}{100}\right)^n$ where $P$ is the principal (original) amount, $r$ is the interest rate and $n$ is the number of times the interest is added on the account.

Sofia puts £100 into a savings account earning 4% interest compounded each year.

Calculate the amount in her savings account after 3 years, assuming she does not make any further deposits.

£ .........................................

## Rearranging a formula to change the subject

**3** The formula for the area of a trapezium is $A = \frac{1}{2}(a + b)h$

   **a)** Rearrange the formula to make $b$ the subject.

.....................................................

   **b)** This trapezium has an area of 78 cm². Work out the length of $b$.

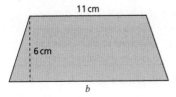

11 cm

6 cm

$b$

$b =$ ......................................... cm

# (2) Algebraic proof

## Proofs involving integers

Algebraic proofs involve using algebra to prove that something is true for all values.

**To write an algebraic proof:**
1. Write down an expression that will show the given statement is always true.
2. Use appropriate methods (e.g. simplifying and rearranging equations) to show the expression is always true.

Some common proofs involving integers will be about even, odd or consecutive numbers.

> An even number can be written as $2n$, where $n$ is an integer. An odd number can be written as $2n + 1$. Consecutive numbers can be written as $n$, $n + 1$, $n + 2$, and so on.

---

Prove that the sum of any two odd numbers is an even number.

Let $n$ and $m$ be integers. ← Start by stating what the variables represent.

Then $2n + 1$ is an odd number and $2m + 1$ is an odd number.

Add the terms.

$(2n + 1) + (2m + 1) = 2n + 2m + 2$

$= 2(n + m + 1)$, which is a multiple of 2.

Factorise.

An even number is a multiple of 2 by definition, so the sum of any two odd numbers is even.

---

Prove that the difference between the squares of any two consecutive odd numbers is always a multiple of 8.

Let $2n + 1$ be an odd number, then $2n + 3$ is a consecutive odd number.

$(2n + 3)^2 - (2n + 1)^2$ ← Write down the problem.

$(2n + 3)^2 = (2n + 3)(2n + 3) = 4n^2 + 12n + 9$

$(2n + 1)^2 = (2n + 1)(2n + 1) = 4n^2 + 4n + 1$

Then $(2n + 3)^2 - (2n + 1)^2 =$
$(4n^2 + 12n + 9) - (4n^2 + 4n + 1)$

$= 8n + 8$ ← Simplify and then factorise.

$= 8(n + 1)$, which is a multiple of 8.

## Proving an identity or algebraic expression

An identity is true for all values whilst an equation is only true for certain values.

> An identity is written with ≡ instead of =

For example, $2x + 3x \equiv 5x$ is an identity. The sum of $2x$ and $3x$ will always be $5x$, no matter what the value of $x$ is. Conversely $2x + 3x = 10$ is an equation. It is only true when $x = 2$.

---

Show that $(2n + 1)^2 - 1 \equiv 4n(n + 1)$

In this example, you need to show that the two sides are equal.

$(2n + 1)^2 - 1 = 4n^2 + 2n + 2n + 1 - 1$

$= 4n^2 + 4n$ ← Simplify. | Expand the brackets.

$= 4n(n + 1)$ ← Factorise.

So, $(2n + 1)^2 - 1 \equiv 4n(n + 1)$ for all values of $n$.

---

Prove that every term in the sequence with $n$th term rule $n^2 - 6n + 10$ is positive.

Show that $n^2 - 6n + 10 > 0$ for any value of $n$.

$n^2 - 6n + 10$

$(n - 3)^2 - 9 + 10$ ← Complete the square (see page 50) on $n^2 - 6n$.

$(n - 3)^2 + 1$

$(n - 3)^2 \geqslant 0$ ← A number squared will always be positive as, even if $n - 3 < 0$, a negative number squared is positive.

So $(n - 3)^2 + 1 > 0$

## Proof by counter-example

You may also be asked to prove that something is **not** true.

---

Belle says that $\frac{1}{n} + \frac{1}{m} = \frac{1}{n + m}$ for any value of $n$ and $m$. Prove that she is **not** correct.

Let $n = 2$ and $m = 3$,

Then $\frac{1}{n} + \frac{1}{m} = \frac{1}{2} + \frac{1}{3} = \frac{3}{6} + \frac{2}{6} = \frac{5}{6}$ ← Evaluate both sides.

and $\frac{1}{n + m} = \frac{1}{2 + 3} = \frac{1}{5}$

$\frac{1}{5} \neq \frac{5}{6}$ ← Give one example that shows the statement is not true.

# (2) Algebraic proof

## Proofs involving integers

**1** Prove that the sum of three consecutive integers is always a multiple of 3.

_____

_____

_____

_____

**2** Prove the product of two odd numbers is always an odd number.

_____

_____

_____

_____

## Proving an identity or algebraic expression

**3** Prove that $a^2 - b^2 \equiv (a + b)(a - b)$

_____

_____

_____

_____

**4** Show that $(x + 1)^2 - 4 = (x - 1)(x + 3)$ for all values of $x$.

_____

_____

_____

_____

## Proof by counter-example

**5** Rhys says that the sum of any two square numbers is also a square number.

Prove that he is incorrect.

_____

_____

_____

_____

_____

# 2  Straight-line graphs

## Drawing straight-line graphs and working out gradients

A **linear** graph is a straight-line graph, e.g. $y = x$, $y = 2x + 3$, $x + y = 5$.

You may be given a table of values to complete before drawing a linear graph.

**To draw a linear graph:**
1. Find three values for $x$ in the range of the graph. $x = 0$ and $y = 0$ are often easy points to use.
2. Plot the points.
3. Connect the points with a straight line.

Draw the graph of $x + y = 5$ for values of $x$ from 0 to 5. Work out the midpoint of the line segment.

For each value of $x$, work out the corresponding $y$ value.

| $x$ | 0 | 2 | 5 |
|---|---|---|---|
| $y$ | 5 | 3 | 0 |

Midpoint $= \left( \frac{x_1 + x_2}{2}, \frac{y_1 + y_2}{2} \right)$
$= \left( \frac{0 + 5}{2}, \frac{5 + 0}{2} \right)$
$= (2.5, 2.5)$

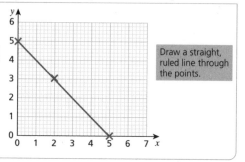

Draw a straight, ruled line through the points.

**To work out the gradient (steepness) of a line:**
1. Find the coordinates of two points on the line.
2. Substitute them into the formula
$\text{Gradient} = \frac{\text{Difference in } y \text{ values}}{\text{Difference in } x \text{ values}}$

When finding the difference between the $x$ and $y$ values, remember to subtract the first $x$ value from the second $x$ value and the first $y$ value from the second $y$ value, or vice-versa.

The gradients of **parallel lines** are equal. The product of the gradients of **perpendicular lines** is –1.

Given the line $y = 3x - 4$:
- The line $y = 3x + 1$ is parallel to the line $y = 3x - 4$ because the gradient of both is 3.
- The line $y = -\frac{1}{3}x - 5$ is perpendicular to the line $y = 3x - 4$ because $-\frac{1}{3} \times 3 = -1$.

Work out the gradient of the straight line.

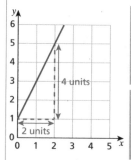

4 units

2 units

The line shown here has a positive gradient. A line going downwards from top left to bottom right (as in the example above) would have a negative gradient.

Two points on the line are (0, 1) and (2, 5). You can use these points to form a triangle that helps you to find the gradient.

$\text{Gradient} = \frac{\text{Difference in } y \text{ values}}{\text{Difference in } x \text{ values}} = \frac{5 - 1}{2 - 0} = \frac{4}{2} = 2$

## $y = mx + c$

Equations of straight lines can be written in the form $y = mx + c$, where $m$ is the gradient and $c$ is the $y$-intercept.

Work out the gradient and the $y$-intercept of the line $x + 2y = 5$.

$2y = 5 - x$
$y = \frac{5}{2} - \frac{x}{2}$
$y = -\frac{1}{2}x + \frac{5}{2}$

Rearrange the equation to make $y$ the subject.

The gradient is $-\frac{1}{2}$ and the $y$-intercept is (0, 2.5).

**To find the equation of a line given two points:**
1. Find the gradient.
2. Substitute the gradient and one of the points into $y = mx + c$ to find the $y$-intercept.
3. Write the equation in the form $y = mx + c$.

Work out the equation of a line passing through the points (–3, 4) and (6,–2).

$\text{Gradient} = \frac{-2 - 4}{6 - (-3)} = \frac{-6}{9} = -\frac{2}{3}$

$y = mx + c$
$4 = \left( -\frac{2}{3} \times -3 \right) + c$
$4 = 2 + c$
$c = 2$

Substitute $m = -\frac{2}{3}$, $y = 4$ and $x = -3$

Equation: $y = -\frac{2}{3}x + 2$

# 2 Straight-line graphs

## Drawing straight-line graphs and working out gradients

**1** Draw the graph of $y = 3x - 3$ for values from $x = 0$ to $x = 4$.

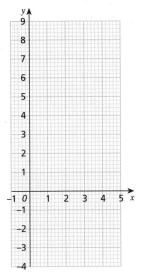

**2** Work out the gradient of the line shown.

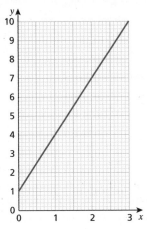

Gradient = ........................

**3** Write down the gradient of a line that is:

**a)** parallel to the line shown in question 2

........................

**b)** perpendicular to the line shown in question 2.

........................

## $y = mx + c$

**4** Work out the gradient and the $y$-intercept of each of the following lines.

**a)** $y - 5 = 2x$

Gradient = ................, $y$-intercept = ................

**b)** $3y - 9 = -4x$

Gradient = ................, $y$-intercept = ................

**5** Write an equation for a line passing through the points (0, 3) and (1, 5).

........................

# ② Quadratic graphs

## Features of a quadratic graph

A **quadratic function** is one where the highest power of $x$ is 2, e.g. $y = x^2 + 4x + 3$.

The graph of a **quadratic function** is a U-shaped **curve** (parabola) upwards $\cup$ or downwards $\cap$.

The **turning point** is the point at which the graph changes from increasing to decreasing or vice-versa. It is the bottom (or top) of the 'U' shape.

A quadratic graph can have no, one or two root(s).

No $x$-intercepts    One $x$-intercept    Two $x$-intercepts

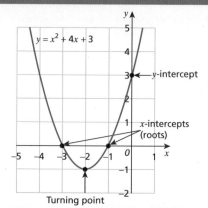

## Drawing the graph of a quadratic equation

To draw the graph of a quadratic equation:

1. Find the $y$-intercept.
2. Find the $x$-intercepts (roots).
3. Find the turning point.
4. Plot the points and connect them with a smooth curve.

> If asked to **sketch** a graph, you need to find the key points, label them and show the general shape of the curve.

**To work out the $y$-intercept:**

Substitute $x = 0$ into the equation and find the value of $y$.

> The $y$-intercept is always the constant value of the equation in the form $y = ax^2 + bx + c$.

$y = x^2 + 4x + 3$
When $x = 0$
$y = 0 + (4 \times 0) + 3$
$y = 3$, so the $y$-intercept is $(0, 3)$.

**To work out the $x$-intercepts algebraically:**

The $x$-intercepts are where $y = 0$, so solve the equation $0 = x^2 + bx + c$ (see page 48 for solving quadratics).

> Solve the equation to find the $x$-intercepts.

$0 = x^2 + 4x + 3$
$0 = (x + 3)(x + 1)$ ← See factorising on page 24.
$x + 3 = 0$ and $x + 1 = 0$ ← Set each bracket equal to 0 and solve.
$x = -3$ and $x = -1$
The $x$-intercepts are $x = -3$ and $x = -1$

**To work out the turning point algebraically:**

1. Complete the square (see page 50) so that the equation is of the form $a(x + h)^2 + k$.
2. The turning point is at the point $(-h, k)$.

$y = x^2 + 4x + 3$
$y = (x + 2)^2 + 3 - 4$
$y = (x + 2)^2 - 1$
The turning point is at $(-2, -1)$.

**To draw a graph by substitution:**

1. Fill in a table of values. Substitute $x$ values into the equation and find the corresponding $y$ values.
2. Plot the points and connect them with a smooth curve.

Here is an example of a table of values for $y = x^2 + 4x + 3$:

| $x$ | −3 | −2 | −1 | 0 | 1 |
|-----|----|----|----|---|---|
| $y$ | 0 | −1 | 0 | 3 | 8 |

# ② Quadratic graphs

## Features of a quadratic graph

**1** The graph of $y = -x^2 + 2x + 8$ is shown.

Write down the coordinates of:

**a)** the y-intercept

.................................

**b)** the x-intercept(s)

.................................

**c)** the turning point.

.................................

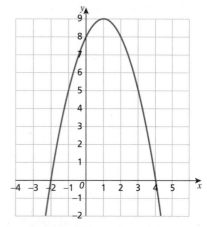

## Drawing the graph of a quadratic equation

**2** For the equation $y + 6x = x^2 + 5$:

**a)** work out the y-intercept

.................................

**b)** work out the x-intercepts

.................................

**c)** work out the turning point

.................................

**d)** draw the graph of the equation.

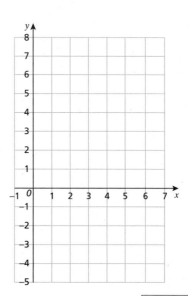

# 2 Other equations and graphs

## Cubic functions

**Cubic functions** have an $x^3$ term as the highest power of $x$, e.g. $y = x^3$ or $y = x^3 - 4$.

Cubic functions may be given in factorised or partly factorised form, e.g. $y = x(x + 3)(x - 2)$.

The general form of a cubic function is given as $y = ax^3 + bx^2 + cx + d$ where $a$, $b$ and $c$ are coefficients and $d$ is a constant.

The general shape of a cubic function is:

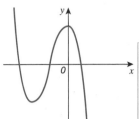

The 'S' shaped curve of a cubic function can intersect the $x$-axis once, twice or three times.

Draw the graph of $y = x^3 - 2$ for values of $x$ from $-2$ to $2$.

Substitute the $x$ values into the equation, e.g. $y = (-2)^3 - 2 = -8 - 2 = -10$

| $x$ | $-2$ | $-1$ | $0$ | $1$ | $2$ |
|---|---|---|---|---|---|
| $y$ | $-10$ | $-3$ | $-2$ | $-1$ | $6$ |

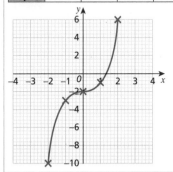

## Reciprocal and exponential functions

**Reciprocal functions** are of the form $y = \frac{k}{x}$ where $x \neq 0$.

**Exponential functions** are of the form $y = k^x$

Make sure you can recognise the general shape of a reciprocal and exponential functions.

To draw graphs of reciprocal and exponential functions:

1. Choose a few values of $x$ and find the corresponding $y$ values.
2. Plot the points and connect them with a smooth curve.

Draw the graph of $y = 2^x$

Substitute the values of $x$, e.g. when $x = 4$, $y = 2^x$ becomes $y = 2^4 = 16$

| $x$ | $0$ | $1$ | $2$ | $3$ | $4$ |
|---|---|---|---|---|---|
| $y$ | $1$ | $2$ | $4$ | $8$ | $16$ |

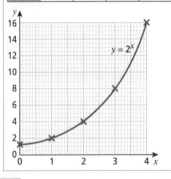

Draw the graph of $y = \frac{1}{x}$ where $x \neq 0$.

Substitute values of $x$ into the equation, e.g. when $x = 3$, $y = \frac{1}{3}$, and when $x = -3$, $y = \frac{1}{-3} = -\frac{1}{3}$

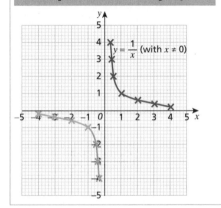

## 2 Other equations and graphs

### Cubic functions

**1** Complete the table of values and draw the graph of $y = x^3 + 1$.

| x | −2 | −1 | 0 | 1 | 2 |
|---|----|----|---|---|---|
| y |    |    |   |   |   |

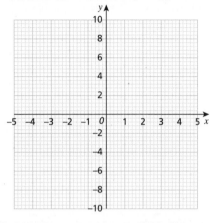

### Reciprocal and exponential functions

**2** Complete the table of values and draw the graph of $y = \frac{3}{x}$

| x | −3 | −2 | −1 | 1 | 2 | 3 |
|---|----|----|----|---|---|---|
| y |    |    |    |   |   |   |

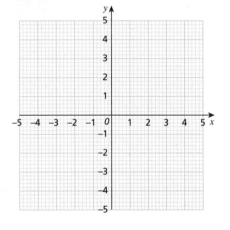

**3** Complete the table of values and draw the graph of $y = 3^x$

| x | −2 | −1 | 0 | 1 | 2 |
|---|----|----|---|---|---|
| y |    |    |   |   |   |

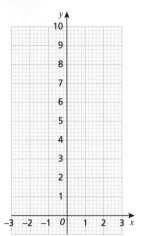

# ② Functions

## Composite functions

A **function** links an input and an output.

Functions are often written using notation such as f(x) or g(x), where x is the input, e.g. $f(x) = x^3 + 2$ or $g(x) = 2x + 1$.

A **composite function** is made by combining two functions. The input of one function is the output of another. The composite function is written as fg(x) to show that the output of g(x) becomes the input of f(x).

fg(x) means apply g(x) first, then use the output as the input of f(x).

$f(x) = 2x + 1$ and $g(x) = x^3$. Work out the value of fg(2).

Work out g(2), then find f(x) using the output.

$g(2) = 2^3 = 8$ ← Substitute 2 in for x.

$fg(2) = (2 \times 8) + 1$ ← Substitute 8 in for x.

$fg(2) = 17$

## Inverse functions

An **inverse function** links the output of a function back to the input. It is written as $f^{-1}(x)$ in function notation.

**To work out the inverse of a function:**
1. Write f(x) as y.
2. Swap the x and y in the equation.
3. Solve for y.
4. Write f(x) for y.

To find the inverse function, rearrange to make x the subject.

$f(x) = 3x - 4$. Work out $f^{-1}(x)$.

$y = 3x - 4$ ← Write f(x) as y.

$x = 3y - 4$ ← Swap x and y.

$x + 4 = 3y$

$\frac{x + 4}{3} = y$ ← Use inverse operations to solve for y.

$f^{-1}(x) = \frac{x + 4}{3}$

Check:

$f(3) = 3 \times 3 - 4 = 5$

$f^{-1}(5) = \frac{5 + 4}{3} = 3 \checkmark$

Substitute a value of x and check that the inverse function 'undoes' it.

## Trigonometric functions

| $y = \sin x$ | • Repeats every 360°<br>• Line of symmetry about x = 90° |
| --- | --- |

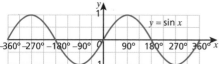

| $y = \cos x$ | • Repeats every 360°<br>• Line of symmetry about x = 0° |
| --- | --- |

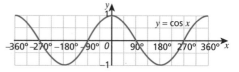

| $y = \tan x$ | • Repeats every 180°<br>• Has vertical asymptotes at 90° ± 180°<br>• Is not a continuous curve |
| --- | --- |

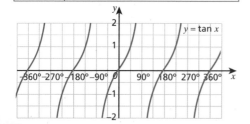

Given that cos 60° = 0.5, use the graph $y = \cos x$ to work out cos 300°.

Use the symmetrical properties of the graph. In this case, use line symmetry with mirror line x = 180°.

$y = \cos x$ has line symmetry about x = 180° so cos 300° = 0.5

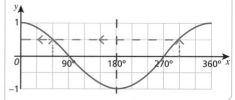

# 2 Functions

## Composite functions

**1** $f(x) = 3x - 1$      $g(x) = x^2$

**a)** Work out $fg(3)$

**b)** Work out $gf(2)$

## Inverse functions

**2** $f(x) = 3x - 1$

Work out $f^{-1}(x)$

**3** $g(x) = 2(x - 1)^2$

Work out $g^{-1}(x)$

## Trigonometric functions

**4** Use the graphs on page 36 to write down approximate values of:

**a)** $\sin 150°$

**b)** $\tan 135°$

# 2 Transformation of functions

The notation $y = f(x)$ is used to represent any graph where $f(x)$ is a function of $x$. Graphs of functions can be transformed by vertical or horizontal movement, or by reflection.

## Vertical and horizontal shifts

**$y = f(x) + a$**

$y = f(x) + a$ is a vertical shift of $y = f(x)$ by $a$ units in the $y$ direction or by the vector $\begin{pmatrix} 0 \\ a \end{pmatrix}$.

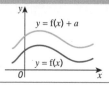

**$y = f(x + a)$**

$y = f(x + a)$ is a horizontal shift of $y = f(x)$ by $-a$ units in the $x$ direction or by the vector $\begin{pmatrix} -a \\ 0 \end{pmatrix}$.

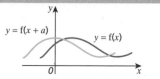

The graph of $y = f(x)$ is shown below left. Draw the graph of $y = f(x) + 3$.

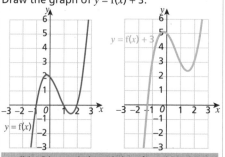

$y = f(x) + 3$ is a vertical translation of $y = f(x)$ by 3 in the $y$ direction.

The graph of $y = f(x)$ is shown below left. Draw the graph of $y = f(x - 2)$.

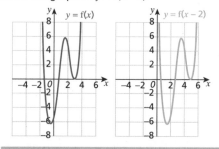

$y = f(x - 2)$ is a horizontal translation by 2 units in the $x$ direction.

## Reflections

**$y = -f(x)$**

$y = -f(x)$ is a reflection of $y = f(x)$ in the $x$-axis.

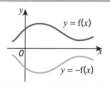

**$y = f(-x)$**

$y = f(-x)$ is a reflection of $y = f(x)$ in the $y$-axis.

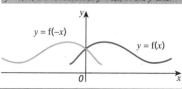

The graph of $y = g(x)$ is shown below left. Draw the graph of $y = g(-x)$.

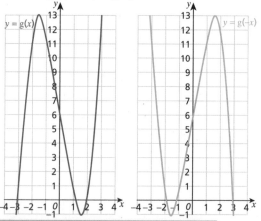

$y = g(-x)$ is a reflection of $g(x)$ in the $y$-axis.

# 2 Transformation of functions

## Vertical and horizontal shifts

**1** The graph of $y = \sin x$ is shown below.

Draw the graph of $y = \sin(x - 90°)$ on the same grid.

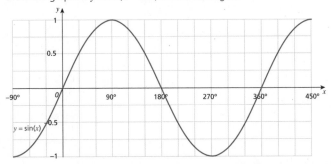

## Reflections

**2** The graph of $y = f(x)$ is shown.

Draw the graph of $y = -f(x)$ on the same grid.

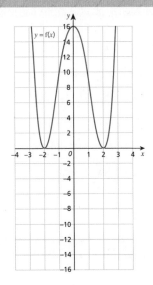

**3** The graph of $y = \cos x$ is shown.

Explain why the graph of $y = \cos(-x)$ is the same.

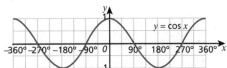

........................................................................................................................

........................................................................................................................

# ② Real-life graphs

## Distance–time graphs

Interpreting graphs in context involves reading values of $x$ or $y$ from the graph. For a linear graph, you can also interpret the gradient as a **rate of change**.

The $y$-intercept represents the starting value and the gradient represents the rate of change. On a distance-time graph, the gradient is the **speed**. On a velocity-time graph, the gradient is the **acceleration**.

The graph shows Sara's journey home from school. She stopped at the library on the way.

*Graph: Distance (miles) on y-axis from 0 to 2, Time (minutes) on x-axis from 0 to 40.*

a) How long did Sara stop at the library?

30 – 15 = 15 minutes

The line is horizontal between 15 and 30 minutes.

b) Work out her average speed from school to the library in miles per hour.

She travels 1 mile in 15 minutes.

Average speed $= \frac{\text{distance travelled}}{\text{time taken}}$

$= 1 \div \frac{1}{4}$

$= 4$ mph          15 minutes $= \frac{1}{4}$ hour

c) What is the distance from school to home?

Home is 2 miles from school.

## Quadratic graphs in context

Quadratic graphs are often used to model motion, such as throwing a ball.

This graph shows the path of a ball thrown from a height.

a) From what height was the ball thrown?

The initial height is the $y$-intercept, which is (0, 2) on this graph.

2 metres

b) After approximately how many seconds did the ball land on the ground?

The $x$-intercept is just before (3, 0).

Approximately 2.8 seconds

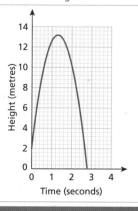

The turning point on this graph represents the maximum height the ball reached.

## Other graphs in context

Graphs of reciprocal, exponential, and trigonometric functions can also be used to model real-life situations.

There is a fixed cost to hire a boat for a day at a lake. A boat can hold up to 12 people.

The graph shows the amount that each person must pay depending on the number of people sharing the cost.

Approximately how much must each person pay if 6 people are sharing the boat?

Draw a line from $x = 6$ to the curve and follow it over to the $y$-axis.

Each person must pay approximately £80.

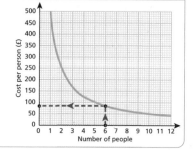

## 2 Real-life graphs

## Distance–time graphs

1 This graph shows Abdul's journey to two shops and back home.

a) For how long did Abdul stop in the two shops in total?

.................................. minutes

b) What was Abdul's average speed on the way home from the shops?

.................................. mph

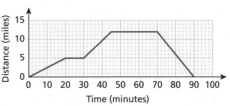

## Quadratic graphs in context

2 This graph shows the profit of a company depending on the number of units sold.

a) How many units must the company sell to maximise profit?

..................................

b) What is the maximum profit?

£ ..................................

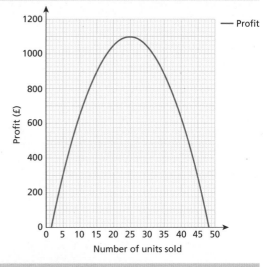

## Other graphs in context

3 A colony of bacteria doubles in number every minute.

After approximately how many minutes does the colony have 6 bacteria?

.................................. minutes

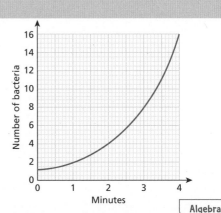

# Gradient at a point on a curve and area under a curve

## Gradient at a point on a curve

The gradient at any particular point on a curve is the **instantaneous rate of change** and represents the rate of change at that particular point in time.

To calculate the gradient ($m$) of a point on a curve, draw a straight line that touches the curve at the desired point (this is called a tangent) and work out the gradient:

$$m = \frac{y_2 - y_1}{x_2 - x_1}$$

To interpret the gradient, divide the units of the $y$-axis by the units of the $x$-axis.

This graph below shows the distance run by an athlete against time. Estimate the instantaneous speed of the runner at 60 minutes. Give your answer in mph to 3 significant figures.

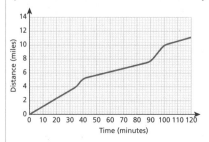

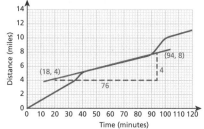

$m = \dfrac{8 - 4}{94 - 18} = \dfrac{4}{76}$ miles per minute

$\dfrac{4}{76} \times 60 = 3.16$ mph (to 3 s.f.)

Multiply by 60 to convert to mph.

## Area under a curve

The area under a curve can be estimated by dividing the space under it into triangles and trapeziums.

You can interpret the area under a curve by multiplying the units of the $y$-axis by the units of the $x$-axis.

This graph shows the speed of a car over time.

Work out the distance the car has travelled after 6 seconds.

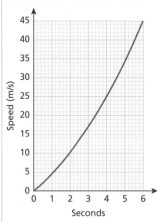

Distance = speed × time so the distance is the area under the curve. Split the area up into triangles and trapeziums.

Area of 1 = $\frac{1}{2} \times 2 \times 10 = 10$

Area of 2 = $\frac{10 + 25}{2} \times 2 = 35$

Area of 3 = $\frac{25 + 45}{2} \times 2 = 70$

Total area = 10 + 35 + 70 = 115

The car travelled 115 metres.

Area of trapezium = $\frac{a + b}{2} \times h$

where $a$ and $b$ are the parallel sides and $h$ is the perpendicular height.

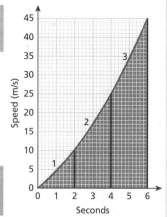

# Gradient at a point on a curve and area under a curve

## Gradient at a point on a curve

**1** The graph is shown of a function, $g(x)$.

Estimate the gradient at the point (1, 0).

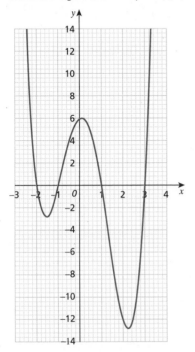

........................................

## Area under a curve

**2** The graph shows the speed (in metres per second) of a cyclist during the first 30 seconds of a sprint race.

Estimate the distance travelled in the first 30 seconds.

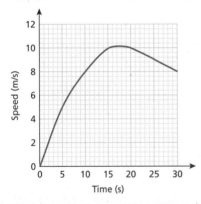

........................................ m

# 2 Graphs of circles

## Graph of a circle

The equation of a graph of a circle with centre $(0, 0)$ is $x^2 + y^2 = r^2$, where $r$ is the radius of the circle.

> To sketch a circle, you need the centre and the radius. Label the points of intersection of the circle and the axes.

> Work out the radius of the circle given by the equation $y^2 = 30 - x^2$.
>
> Rearrange the equation.
>
> $x^2 + y^2 = 30$
>
> The value of $r^2 = 30$, so the radius is $\sqrt{30}$.

a) Sketch the graph of a circle with centre $(0, 0)$ and radius 4.

> Draw a circle with radius of 4, making sure it crosses the axes at $(-4, 0)$, $(4, 0)$, $(0, -4)$ and $(0, 4)$.

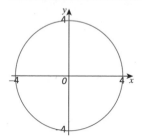

b) Write down the equation of the graph.

> The general equation of a circle is $x^2 + y^2 = r^2$

The equation is $x^2 + y^2 = 16$

## The equation of the tangent to the circle at a point

A **tangent** is a straight line that just touches the circle at one point on the circumference. It is perpendicular to the radius at that point.

> The tangent and radius are perpendicular, so the product of the gradient of the tangent and the gradient of the radius is $-1$.

**To work out the equation of the tangent at a given point:**

1. Draw the tangent at the point on the circle.
2. Draw the radius from the centre of the circle to the point.
3. Calculate the gradient of the radius.
4. Use the gradient of the radius to find the gradient of the tangent.
5. Substitute the gradient of the tangent and the coordinates of the given point into $y = mx + c$ and rearrange to find $c$.
6. Write the equation of the tangent.

Work out the equation of the tangent to the circle $x^2 + y^2 = 100$ at the point $(6, 8)$.

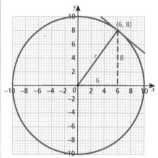

The gradient of the radius is $m = \frac{8}{6} = \frac{4}{3}$ so the gradient of the tangent is $-\frac{3}{4}$

$\frac{4}{3} \times -\frac{3}{4} = -1$

$y = mx + c$

$8 = \left(-\frac{3}{4} \times 6\right) + c$

Substitute $(6, 8)$ and $m = -\frac{3}{4}$

$8 = -\frac{9}{2} + c$

$8 + \frac{9}{2} = c$

Solve for $c$.

$c = \frac{25}{2}$

The equation of the tangent is $y = -\frac{3}{4}x + \frac{25}{2}$

# Graphs of circles

## Graph of a circle

**1** Sketch graphs of the following circles.

**a)** $x^2 + y^2 = 9$

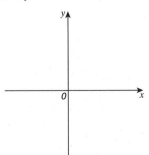

**b)** $x^2 + y^2 = 4$

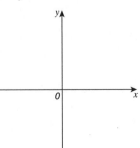

**c)** $x^2 + y^2 = 2$

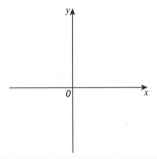

## The equation of the tangent to the circle at a point

**2** The circle with equation $x^2 + y^2 = 18$ is shown.

Work out the equation of the tangent at (3, 3).

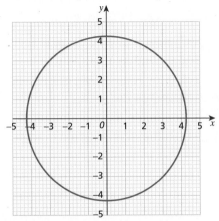

## ② Solving linear equations

### Multi-step equations

To solve equations, use inverse operations to isolate the variable.

> Whatever you do to one side of the equation, you must also do to the other side.

a) **Solve** $2x + 3 = 11$

$$2x \; \boxed{\begin{array}{c} +3 \\ -3 \end{array}} = 11 \\ -3$$

$$2x = 8$$

$$\frac{2x}{2} = \frac{8}{2}$$

$$x = 4$$

Subtract 3 from both sides of the equation to leave just the $x$ term on the left-hand side. Note that +3 and –3 give a zero, shown by the circle.

Divide both sides by 2 to leave just $x$ on the left-hand side.

b) **Solve** $8x - 5 = 4x + 3$

$$8x \; \boxed{\begin{array}{c} -5 \\ +5 \end{array}} = 4x \quad +3 \\ +5$$

$$8x = \boxed{4x} + 8 \\ -4x \quad -4x$$

$$4x = 8$$

$$\frac{4x}{4} = \frac{8}{4}$$

$$x = 2$$

Add 5 to both sides of the equation to leave just the $x$ term on the left-hand side. Note that –5 and +5 give a zero, shown by the circle.

Subtract $4x$ from both sides of the equation to leave just the number 8 on the right-hand side.

Divide both sides by 4 to leave just $x$ on the left-hand side.

### Linear equations with brackets

To solve equations with brackets, first expand the brackets, then solve.

**Solve** $6(2x - 1) = 5(2x + 4)$

$$12x - 6 = 10x + 20$$

$$12x \; \boxed{\begin{array}{c} -6 \\ +6 \end{array}} = 10x + 20 \\ +6$$

$$12x = \boxed{10x} + 26 \\ -10x \quad -10x$$

$$2x = 26$$

$$\frac{2x}{2} = \frac{26}{2}$$

$$x = 13$$

Multiply out the brackets on both sides.

Add 6 to both sides of the equation to leave just the $x$ term on the left-hand side.

Subtract $10x$ from both sides of the equation to leave just the number 26 on the right-hand side.

Divide both sides by 2 to leave just $x$ on the left-hand side.

## ② Solving linear equations

### Multi-step equations

**1** Solve each equation.

**a)** $8 - 3x = -4$

**b)** $5x - 2 = 3x + 4$

$x =$ ........................................

$x =$ ........................................

**c)** $3x - 12 = x - 4$

**d)** $18 = 6 - 3x$

$x =$ ........................................

$x =$ ........................................

### Linear equations with brackets

**2** Solve each equation.

**a)** $3(x - 4) = 2x - 15$

**b)** $2(3x + 4) = 2(4x - 1)$

$x =$ ........................................

$x =$ ........................................

**c)** $2(x - 3) = 9 - x$

**d)** $3(x - 1) = 2(2x - 5)$

$x =$ ........................................

$x =$ ........................................

# ② Solving quadratic equations

## Quadratic equations of the form $x^2 + bx + c = 0$

**To solve a quadratic equation by factorising:**
1. Rearrange the equation into the form $x^2 + bx + c = 0$.
2. Factorise $x^2 + bx + c$.
3. Set each bracket equal to zero.
4. Solve the linear equations.

---

Solve $x^2 - 5x + 6 = 0$

The equation is already in the form $x^2 + bx + c = 0$

$x^2 - 5x + 6 = 0$

$(x - 2)(x - 3) = 0$

So $x - 2 = 0$ or $x - 3 = 0$

$x = 2$ or $x = 3$

---

To solve after factorising, set each bracket equal to zero and solve for $x$.

---

The solutions of a quadratic are $x = 2$ and $x = -4$.

Work out the equation.

To obtain the quadratic equation, work backwards from the solutions.

$x = 2$ and $x = -4$

So $x - 2 = 0$ or $x + 4 = 0$ ← Set up the linear equations.

So $(x - 2)(x + 4) = 0$ ← Combine the equations to from a quadratic.

$x^2 + 2x - 8 = 0$ ← Expand the brackets.

## Quadratic equations of the form $ax^2 + bx + c = 0$

**To solve equations of the form $ax^2 + bx + c = 0$:**
1. Rearrange the equation into the form $ax^2 + bx + c = 0$.
2. Check if there is a common factor of all three terms; if there is, divide by it.
3. Factorise the quadratic expression.
4. Set each bracket equal to zero.
5. Solve the linear equations.

---

Always check for a common factor first. It might make the problem easier.

---

A rectangle has length $(2x + 3)$ cm and a width of $(x - 2)$ cm. It has an area of 39 cm².

Work out the value of $x$.

$(2x + 3)(x - 2) = 2x^2 - x - 6$ ← Write an expression for the area.

$2x^2 - x - 6 = 39$

$2x^2 - x - 45 = 0$ ← Set the expression equal to zero and solve.

$2x^2 - 10x + 9x - 45 = 0$ ← $9x \times -10x = -90x$ and $9x - 10x = -x$

$2x(x - 5) + 9(x - 5) = 0$

$(2x + 9)(x - 5) = 0$

$2x + 9 = 0 \rightarrow x = -4.5$ (which cannot be as the rectangle would have a negative length and width)

Or $\quad x - 5 = 0 \rightarrow x = 5$

---

Solve the equation $3x^2 = 6 - 3x$

First rearrange the equation into the form $ax^2 + bx + c = 0$.

$3x^2 + 3x - 6 = 0$

$3(x^2 + x - 2) = 0$ ← Take out the common factor of 3.

$(x - 1)(x + 2) = 0$ ← Divide both sides by 3.

$x - 1 = 0 \qquad$ or $\qquad x + 2 = 0$

$x = 1 \qquad$ or $\qquad x = -2$

---

Solve $2x^2 + 7x - 4 = 0$

$2x^2 + 7x - 4 = 0$

$(2x - 1)(x + 4) = 0$

So $2x - 1 = 0$ or $x + 4 = 0$

$2x = 1$ or $x = -4$

$x = \frac{1}{2}$ or $x = -4$

$-1x$ and $8x$ multiply to $-8x^2$ and add to $7x$

$2x^2 + 7x - 4 = (2x - 1)(x + 4)$

## ② Solving quadratic equations

### Quadratic equations of the form $x^2 + bx + c = 0$

**1** Solve each equation.

**a)** $x^2 - 5x = 24$

**b)** $x^2 = 15 - 2x$

$x =$ .........................................

$x =$ .........................................

**c)** $x^2 = -4x - 4$

**d)** $x^2 - 6 = x$

$x =$ .........................................

$x =$ .........................................

### Quadratic equations of the form $ax^2 + bx + c = 0$

**2** Solve each equation.

**a)** $6 - 9x = -3x^2$

**b)** $2x^2 - 5x = 12$

$x =$ .........................................

$x =$ .........................................

**c)** $2x^2 = 3x + 2$

**d)** $5x^2 + 2 = 7x$

$x =$ .........................................

$x =$ .........................................

# Completing the square and the quadratic formula

## Completing the square

To **complete the square** on quadratic expression means to write it in the form $(x - h)^2 + k$.

**To complete the square:**
1. Rearrange the expression to be in the form $x^2 + bx + c$.
2. Divide the $b$ term by 2 and write the expression as $\left(x + \frac{b}{2}\right)^2 - \left(\frac{b}{2}\right)^2 + c$.
3. Simplify.

Don't forget to subtract $\left(\frac{b}{2}\right)^2$ and to include the $c$ value.

**To solve a quadratic by completing the square:**
1. Complete the square so the equation is of the form $(x - h)^2 + k = 0$.
2. Solve the equation using inverse operations.

Solve $x^2 - 10x + 9 = 0$ for $x$ by completing the square.

$(x - 5)^2 - (-5)^2 + 9 = 0$ ← $b = -10$ so $\frac{b}{2} = \frac{-10}{2} = -5$

$(x - 5)^2 - 25 + 9 = 0$

$(x - 5)^2 - 16 = 0$

$x - 5 = \pm\sqrt{16}$ ← Take the square root of both sides.

$x - 5 = \pm 4$ ← $\pm\sqrt{16} = \pm 4$

$x = 5 \pm 4$

$x = 5 + 4$    or    $x = 5 - 4$

$x = 9$    or    $x = 1$

Solve $x^2 - 8x = 6$ by completing the square.

$x^2 - 8x - 6 = 0$ ← Rearrange.

$(x - 4)^2 - 16 - 6 = 0$ ← $\frac{b}{2} = \frac{8}{2} = 4$

$(x - 4)^2 - 22 = 0$

$(x - 4)^2 = 22$ ← Take the square root of both sides. Don't forget the square root can be positive or negative.

$x - 4 = \pm\sqrt{22}$

$x = 4 \pm \sqrt{22}$ ← Answer in surd form.

$x = 8.69$ or $x = -0.69$ (to 2 d.p.)

## The quadratic formula

Any quadratic equation can be solved using the formula:

$$x = \frac{-b \pm \sqrt{b^2 - 4ac}}{2a}$$

**To solve using the quadratic formula:**
1. Rearrange to the form $ax^2 + bx + c = 0$
2. Substitute the values of $a$, $b$ and $c$ into the formula.

Solve $5x^2 + 2x - 4 = 0$

Give your answer to 2 decimal places. ← This is a clue that the quadratic will not factorise.

Substitute for $a$, $b$ and $c$ in the formula.

$a = 5$, $b = 2$, $c = -4$

So $x = \dfrac{-(2) \pm \sqrt{(2)^2 - 4 \times (5) \times (-4)}}{2 \times (5)}$

$x = \dfrac{-2 \pm \sqrt{4 + 80}}{10}$

$x = \dfrac{-2 \pm \sqrt{84}}{10}$

$x = \dfrac{-2 + \sqrt{84}}{10}$ or $x = \dfrac{-2 - \sqrt{84}}{10}$

$x = 0.72$ or $x = -1.12$

# Completing the square and the quadratic formula

## Completing the square

**1** Solve each equation by completing the square. Give your answer in exact form.

**a)** $x^2 - 5 = 4x$

$x =$ .................... or $x =$ ....................

**b)** $x^2 - 8x = 10$

$x =$ ....................

**c)** $x^2 + 26 = 12x$

$x =$ ....................

## The quadratic formula

**2** Solve the equation $3x^2 + 4x + 4 = 5$. Give your answer to 2 decimal places.

$x =$ .................... or $x =$ ....................

# 2 Simultaneous equations

## Solving simultaneous equations by substitution and elimination

To solve a pair of simultaneous equations means to find a solution that works for both equations.

**To solve by substitution:**
1. Rearrange one equation into the form $y = ...$ or $x = ...$
2. Substitute for $y$ or $x$ in the other equation.
3. Solve the equation in the remaining variable.
4. Substitute this value back into the rearranged equation and solve.
5. Check that your solutions satisfy both of the original equations.

> Substitution is a good method to use if the coefficient of one of the variables is 1.

**To solve by elimination:**
1. Multiply one or both of the equations to match the coefficient of one of the variables.
2. Eliminate this variable by adding or subtracting the equations.
3. Solve the linear equation of the remaining variable.
4. Substitute this value back into one of the original equations and solve.
5. Check that your solutions satisfy both of the original equations.

> If the signs on the coefficient are the same, subtract one equation from the other. If the signs are different, add the equations.

Solve the simultaneous equations
$3x + 2y = 7$ and $x - y = -1$.

$3x + 2y = 7$ (1) ← Number the equations (1) and (2) to keep track of your workings.
$x - y = -1$ (2)
$x = -1 + y$ (3) ← Rearrange equation (2) into the form $x = ...$
$3(-1 + y) + 2y = 7$ ← Substitute equation (3) for $x$ in equation (1).
$-3 + 3y + 2y = 7$
$5y = 10$, so $y = 2$
$x = -1 + y$
$x = -1 + 2$, so $x = 1$ ← Substitute $y = 2$ into one of the equations and solve.
Solutions are $x = 1$ and $y = 2$

> Substitute the values of $x$ and $y$ into the original equations and check they work.

Check: $3x + 2y = 7$    $3 + 4 = 7$ ✓
       $x - y = -1$    $1 - 2 = -1$ ✓

> Simultaneous equations involving a quadratic equation can be solved algebraically using substitution.

Solve the simultaneous equations
$5x + 3y = 12$ and $3x + 2y = 7$.

$5x + 3y = 12$ (1) ← Number the equations, e.g. (1) and (2).
$3x + 2y = 7$ (2)
(1) × 2 = $10x + 6y = 24$ (3) ← Multiply equation (1) by 2 and equation (2) by 3 to get the coefficient of $y$ to be 6.
(2) × 3 = $9x + 6y = 21$ (4)
$10x + 6y = 24$
$- (9x + 6y = 21)$ ← Line up the terms and subtract equation (4) from equation (3) to eliminate the $y$ term.
$x = 3$
$3x + 2y = 7$
$(3 × 3) + 2y = 7$ ← Substitute $x = 3$ into (2).
$9 + 2y = 7$
$2y = -2$ ← Subtract 9 from both sides.
$y = -1$
Check: $5x + 3y = 12$    $15 - 3 = 12$ ✓
       $3x + 2y = 7$    $9 - 2 = 7$ ✓

## Solving simultaneous equations graphically

**To solve simultaneous equations graphically:**
1. Draw the graphs of both equations.
2. Find the points of intersection – those are the solutions.

The same applies when solving simultaneous equations involving a quadratic or other non-linear equation.

Solve $x + y = 5$ and $2x + y = 7$.

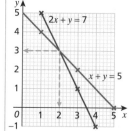

Point of intersection is (2, 3).

Solutions are $x = 2$ and $y = 3$

Check: $x + y = 5$    $2 + 3 = 5$ ✓
       $2x + y = 7$    $4 + 3 = 7$ ✓

## ② Simultaneous equations

## Solving simultaneous equations by substitution and elimination

**1** Solve the following pairs of simultaneous equations.

**a)** $4x - y = 1$

$y + 3 = 2x$

**b)** $2x + 3y = 9$

$4x - 9y = 3$

$x = $ ......................

$y = $ ......................

$x = $ ......................

$y = $ ......................

## Solving simultaneous equations graphically

**2** Write down approximate solutions to each pair of simultaneous equations.

**a)** $x - 4y = 5$

$2x + 5y = -3$

**b)** $y - x = 6$

$y = 2x^2$

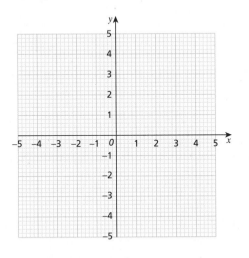

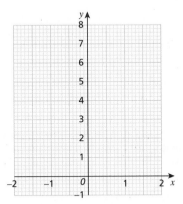

$x = $ ......................

$y = $ ......................

$x = $ .................., $y = $ ..................

$x = $ .................., $y = $ ..................

# 2 Solving equations by iteration

## Solving quadratics by iteration

You can find approximate roots (solutions) to equations using an **iterative formula**. Iterative means to repeatedly carry out an action.

**One way to work out an iterative formula:**
1. Rearrange the equation to leave $x$ on its own.
2. Take any required roots so that the power of $x$ is 1.

To solve an equation using an iterative process:
1. Find an iterative formula (if it is not given).
2. Start with an initial value of $x_0$ (this will often be given to you). The iterative process will usually work towards the solution no matter what starting value you use.
3. Substitute the initial value into the equation; this gives you the value $x_1$.
4. Write down the value $x_1$ and round it to one more than the desired number of decimal places.
5. Use your calculator to substitute the exact value of $x_1$ into the equation, resulting in $x_2$. Do **not** substitute the rounded value of $x_1$.
6. Write down the value of $x_2$ and round it to one more than the desired number of decimal places.
7. Substitute the exact value of $x_2$ into the equation, resulting in $x_3$ and so on.
8. Repeatedly substitute the outcomes into the equation until the rounded output to two successive inputs is the same.
9. The repeated value is the solution to the equation rounded to the required number of decimal places.

Write an iterative formula to work out the roots of $y = x^2 - x - 1$.

$0 = x^2 - x - 1$ ← Substitute $y = 0$ to find the roots.

$x^2 = x + 1$ ← Make $x^2$ the subject.

$x = \sqrt{x + 1}$ ← Take the square root of both sides.

$x_1 = \sqrt{x_0 + 1}$ so $x_{n+1} = \sqrt{x_n + 1}$ ← Write down the iterative formula.

Calculate the positive root to $y = x^2 - x - 1$ to 2 d.p. using the iterative formula $x_{n+1} = \sqrt{x_n + 1}$.

Let $x_0 = 1$ ← State the initial value.

Then $x_1 = \sqrt{1 + 1} = 1.414$ to 3 d.p.

So $x_2 = \sqrt{x_1 + 1} = 1.554$ to 3 d.p.

$x_3 = \sqrt{x_2 + 1} = 1.598$ to 3 d.p.

$x_4 = \sqrt{x_3 + 1} = 1.612$ to 3 d.p.

$x_5 = \sqrt{x_4 + 1} = 1.616$ to 3 d.p.

$x_6 = \sqrt{x_5 + 1} = 1.617$ to 3 d.p.

$x_7 = \sqrt{x_6 + 1} = 1.618$ to 3 d.p.

$x_8 = \sqrt{x_7 + 1} = 1.618$ to 3 d.p.

Use the ANS button on your calculator. Input $\sqrt{ANS + 1}$ and write down the rounded answer.

You can keep pressing = on your calculator and just record the rounded answer until it is the same twice in a row.

The positive root is 1.62 to 2 d.p.

Stop here as the output is 1.618 to 3 decimal places for $x_7$ and $x_8$.

Substitute the exact value in each iteration, not the rounded value.

## Solving higher powers by iteration

Use the same process to find roots of higher powers by iteration.

Calculate the negative root of $y = x^3 - x^2 - 2x + 1$ to 3 decimal places using an iterative formula.

**Work out the iterative formula:**

$0 = x^3 - x^2 - 2x + 1$ ← Substitute $y = 0$ to find the roots.

$x^3 = x^2 + 2x - 1$ ← Make $x^3$ the subject.

$x = \sqrt[3]{x^2 + 2x - 1}$

$x_{n+1} = \sqrt[3]{x_n^2 + 2x_n - 1}$ ← Write down the iterative formula.

**Solve using iteration:**

Let $x_0 = 0$ then $x_1 = \sqrt[3]{0^2 + (2 \times 0) - 1} = -1$

$x_2 = \sqrt[3]{ANS^2 + (2 \times ANS) - 1} = -1.2599$ to 4 d.p.

$x_3 = -1.2456$ to 4 d.p.

$x_4 = -1.2471$ to 4 d.p.

$x_5 = -1.2470$ to 4 d.p.

$x_6 = -1.2470$ to 4 d.p.

You can keep pressing = on your calculator and just record the rounded answer.

Stop here as the output is -1.2470 to 4 decimal places for $x_5$ and $x_6$.

The negative root is -1.247 to 3 d.p.

## 2 Solving equations by iteration

### Solving quadratics by iteration

**1 a)** Show that $x^2 - x - 5 = 0$ can be rearranged to $x = \sqrt{x + 5}$

...............................................................................................................................................

...............................................................................................................................................

...............................................................................................................................................

**b)** Show that $x^3 - x^2 - 3x + 2 = 0$ can be rearranged to $x = \sqrt[3]{x^2 + 3x - 2}$

...............................................................................................................................................

...............................................................................................................................................

...............................................................................................................................................

**2** Use the iterative formula $x_{n+1} = \sqrt{x_n + 5}$ to calculate the positive root of $y = x^2 - x - 5$ to 2 decimal places. Use a starting value of $x_0 = 1$.

$x = $ ...............................

### Solving higher powers by iteration

**3** Use the iterative formula $x_{n+1} = \sqrt[3]{x_n^2 + 3x_n - 2}$ to calculate the negative root of $y = x^3 - x^2 - 3x + 2$ to 3 decimal places. Use a starting value of $x_0 = -2$.

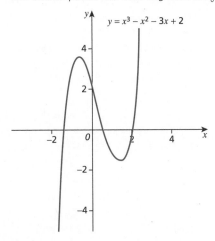

$y = x^3 - x^2 - 3x + 2$

$x = $ ...............................

# 2 Writing and solving equations in context

## Linear equations

You will need to write and solve linear equations in a variety of contexts, such as in geometrical problems or when using rates of change.

> Writing a linear equation often involves simplifying more than one term and solving the equation in context.

A plumber charges a call-out fee of £50 plus £80 per hour.

a) Write an equation to work out the total cost of hiring the plumber.

$T = 50 + 80x$ where $x$ is the number of hours and $T$ is the total cost, in pounds.

b) The plumber takes 3 hours to do a job. Work out the total cost.

$T = 50 + (80 \times 3)$ ◄— Substitute $x = 3$

$= 50 + 240 = £290$

c) The plumber charges £730 for a job. How long did the job take?

$730 = 50 + 80x$

$680 = 80x$ ◄— Subtract 50 from both sides.

$x = 680 \div 80 = 8.5$ ◄— Divide both sides by 80.

The job took 8.5 hours.

Here is an isosceles triangle, ABC.

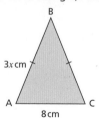

a) Write an equation for the perimeter of the triangle.

$P = 3x + 3x + 8$ ◄— Add up all the sides.

$P = (6x + 8)$ cm

b) The perimeter is 32 cm. Work out the value of $x$.

$6x + 8 = 32$ ◄— Substitute $P = 32$

$6x = 24$ ◄— Subtract 8 from both sides.

$x = 4$ ◄— Divide both sides by 6.

c) Work out the length of each side.

Given $x = 4$, then $3x = 3 \times 4 = 12$

The sides are 12 cm, 12 cm and 8 cm.

## Quadratic equations

An area problem may require you to solve a quadratic equation.

Here is a rectangular garden.

$(x + 3)$ m

$(x + 2)$ m

a) Write an equation for the area of the garden. Give your answer in expanded form.

$A = (x + 2)(x + 3)$ ◄— $A = l \times w$

$A = x^2 + 2x + 3x + 6$ ◄— Expand the brackets.

$A = x^2 + 5x + 6$ ◄— Simplify.

b) The area of the garden is 90 m². Work out the value of $x$.

$x^2 + 5x + 6 = 90$ ◄— Substitute $A = 90$

$x^2 + 5x - 84 = 0$ ◄— Rearrange.

$(x + 12)(x - 7) = 0$ ◄— Factorise.

$x + 12 = 0$ or $x - 7 = 0$ ◄— Set brackets to equal 0.

$x = -12$ or $x = 7$

$x$ cannot be −12 because the dimensions would be negative (if $x = -12$, then $x + 3 = -12 + 3 = -9$).

$x$ must be 7.

c) Work out the dimensions of the garden.

Given $x = 7$, then $x + 2 = 7 + 2 = 9$ and $x + 3 = 7 + 3 = 10$ ◄— Substitute $x = 7$ into each length.

9 m by 10 m

## 2 Writing and solving equations in context

## Linear equations

**1** Here is a triangle.

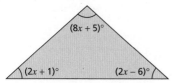

**a)** Write an equation for the sum of the angles in the triangle.

............................................

**b)** Use your answer to part a) to work out the value of $x$.

$x =$ ......................

**c)** Work out the size of each angle in the triangle.

...................... °, ...................... ° and ...................... °.

## Quadratic equations

**2** Here is a parallelogram.

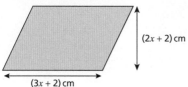

**a)** Write an equation in terms of $x$ for the area of the parallelogram.

............................................

**b)** The area of the parallelogram is 88 cm².

Use the quadratic formula to work out the possible value(s) of $x$.

$x =$ ...................... or $x =$ ......................

**c)** Work out the dimensions of each side.

...................... cm and ...................... cm

# ② Solving and graphing inequalities

## Inequalities on a number line

**Inequalities** use the symbols:

$<$ to mean 'less than'

$>$ to mean 'greater than'

$\leqslant$ to mean 'less than or equal to'

$\geqslant$ to mean 'greater than or equal to'.

The solution to an inequality can be shown on a number line using open (O) and closed circles (●):

means $x <$

means $x >$

means $x \leqslant$

means $x \geqslant$

**Show each of these inequalities on a number line.**

a) $x < 1$

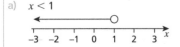

b) $-2 \leqslant x < 5$

Integer solutions are $-2, -1, 0, 1, 2, 3, 4.$

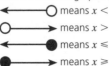

## Solving inequalities

**To solve a linear inequality:**

1. Use the same techniques as when solving an equation.
2. Always collect terms so that the $x$ term has a positive coefficient.
3. Rewrite the answer with $x$ on the left-hand side if needed.

Keep the $x$ term (or other variable) positive and never replace the inequality symbol with an equals sign.

a) Solve $3x - 3 \geqslant x + 7$

$3x - 3 \geqslant x + 7$ — Subtract $x$ from both sides.

$2x - 3 \geqslant 7$ — Add 3 to both sides.

$2x \geqslant 10$ — Divide both sides by 2.

$x \geqslant 5$

b) Solve $-2x > 6$

$-2x > 6$ — Subtract 6 from both sides.

$-6 - 2x > 0$ — Add $2x$ to both sides.

$-6 > 2x$

$-3 > x$ or

$x < -3$ — If $-3$ is greater than $x$, then $x$ is less than $-3$.

c) Solve $6 < 3x \leqslant 12$

Split into two inequalities and solve.

$6 < 3x \leqslant 12$

$6 < 3x$ and $3x \leqslant 12$

$2 < x$        $x \leqslant 4$

$2 < x \leqslant 4$ — Write as a compound inequality.

3 and 4 are integer solutions that satisfy the inequality.

## Graphing inequalities

A linear inequality can be shown by a region on a graph. The region will lie on the side of the straight-line graph for the corresponding equation.

**To graph an inequality:**

1. Draw the straight-line graph for the equation.
2. Use a dotted line for $x >$ or $x <$ to show the points on the line are not included in the solution.
3. Use a solid line for $x \geqslant$ or $x \leqslant$ to show the points on the line are included.
4. Shade the corresponding area on the graph.

To graph a quadratic inequality, shade above or below the curve depending on the inequality sign.

Show graphically the region, R, that satisfies $x \leqslant 2$, $y \geqslant x$ and $y < 2x$.

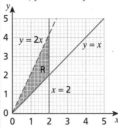

Check your answer by choosing a point in the region and testing that it satisfies all the inequalities.

e.g. (1.5, 2.5) is in the region, R, and $x = 1.5$, $y = 2.5$ obeys all three inequalities.

$x \leqslant 2$, $y \geqslant x$ and $y < 2x$ — $1.5 < 2$, $2.5 > 1.5$ and $2.5 < 3$

# 2 Solving and graphing inequalities

## Inequalities on a number line

**1** Show each inequality on the number line.

**a)** $x < 2$

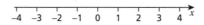

**b)** $x \geq -1$

**c)** $-2 < x \leq 3$

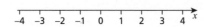

## Solving inequalities

**2 a)** Solve $3x + 2 < 8$

**b)** Solve $2x + 1 \leq 3x + 2$

## Graphing inequalities

**3 a)** Shade the region that satisfies the inequality $y < 2x + 1$.

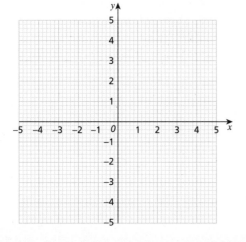

**b)** Shade the region that satisfies the inequalities $x \leq 3$, $y < 2x + 1$ and $y > 2$.

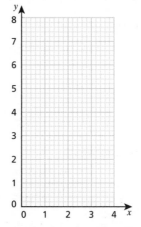

# ② Linear sequences

## Vocabulary

A **sequence** is a set of numbers with a rule to find each number.

A **linear sequence** (or an **arithmetic sequence**) increases or decreases by the same amount from one term to the next.

A **term-to-term rule** is a rule that links one term to the next term.

The **$n$th term rule** (or **position-to-term rule**) links the position of the term to the value of the term.

The sequence of odd numbers is 1, 3, 5, 7, 9, ....

The term-to-term rule is: Start with 1 and add 2.

The position-to-term rule is: Double the position number and subtract 1 (so the $n$th term rule is $2n - 1$).

| Position | 1 | 2 | 3 | 4 | 5 |
|---|---|---|---|---|---|
| Term | 1 | 3 | 5 | 7 | 9 |

## Using the $n$th term rule

The $n$th term rule can be used to find the value of any term in a sequence.

To find the value, substitute the term number for $n$ in the $n$th term rule.

> You can use the $n$th term rule to find any term in the sequence.

Work out the 1st, 2nd, 3rd and 10th terms of the sequence with $n$th term rule $2n - 3$.

When $n = 1$: $(2 \times 1) - 3 = -1$

When $n = 2$: $(2 \times 2) - 3 = 1$

When $n = 3$: $(2 \times 3) - 3 = 3$

When $n = 10$: $(2 \times 10) - 3 = 17$

## Working out the $n$th term rule

The $n$th term of a sequence is a formula for the position-to-term rule, e.g. the formula for the $n$th term for odd numbers would be $2n - 1$.

**To work out the $n$th term rule:**

1. Find the common difference between each term of the sequence.
2. Write down the times table of the common difference.
3. Compare the times table and the terms to work out which number to add or subtract to get the term.
4. Write down the $n$th term rule.

> A table can help to organise your workings.

Work out the $n$th term rule of the sequence 7, 10, 13, 16, 19, ...

The common difference is +3

7    10    13    16    19     So the sequence is linked to the 3 times table.

$+3$   $+3$   $+3$   $+3$

| Position | 1 | 2 | 3 | 4 | 5 |
|---|---|---|---|---|---|
| 3 times table | 3 | 6 | 9 | 12 | 15 |
|  | $+4$ | $+4$ | $+4$ | $+4$ | $+4$ |
| Term | 7 | 10 | 13 | 16 | 19 |

To get from the 3 times tables to the sequence, add 4.

To get from the position to the term, multiply the position by 3 then add 4.

The $n$th term rule is $3n + 4$.

Work out the $n$th term of this sequence:

11, 9, 7, 5, ...

The term-to-term rule is 'subtract 2'.

11    9    7    5    So the sequence is linked to the 2 times table.

$-2$   $-2$   $-2$

So the $n$th term will be of the form $-2n + c$.

When $n = 1$: $\quad -2 \times 1 + c = 11$, so $c = 13$

So the $n$th term is $-2n + 13$ or $13 - 2n$.

## 2 Linear sequences

## Vocabulary

**1** For each sequence, work out the term-to-term rule and the next **two** terms.

**a)** 2, 7, 12, 17, _____, _____

Term-to-term rule: _____

**b)** 12, 8, 4, 0, _____, _____

Term-to-term rule: _____

## Using the $n$th term rule

**2** Work out the 1st, 2nd, 3rd and 10th term of the sequence with $n$th term rule:

**a)** $4n + 5$

1st term: _____  2nd term: _____  3rd term: _____  10th term: _____

**b)** $2 - 5n$

1st term: _____  2nd term: _____  3rd term: _____  10th term: _____

## Working out the $n$th term rule

**3** Work out the $n$th term for each sequence.

**a)** 5, 7, 9, 11, 13, …

**b)** 17, 14, 11, 8, …

# ② Other types of sequences

## Geometric sequences

In a **geometric sequence**, each term is multiplied by a **common ratio** to get the next term.

To find the common ratio, divide any two consecutive terms. It is a good idea to check a second set of consecutive terms.

a) Work out the term-to-term rule for the sequence 2, 4, 8, 16, 32, ...

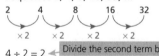

| 2 | 4 | 8 | 16 | 32 |

×2    ×2    ×2    ×2

$4 \div 2 = 2$ ← Divide the second term by the first.

$8 \div 4 = 2$ ← Check by dividing the third term by the second.

The term-to-term rule is start at 2 and multiply by 2.

b) Work out the missing term of the sequence 640, 160, 40, ____, 2.5

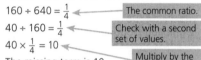

$160 \div 640 = \frac{1}{4}$ ← The common ratio.

$40 \div 160 = \frac{1}{4}$ ← Check with a second set of values.

$40 \times \frac{1}{4} = 10$ ← Multiply by the common ratio.

The missing term is 10.

a) Work out the common ratio in the sequence 500, 100, 20, 4, ...

$100 \div 500 = \frac{1}{5}$ ← Divide the second term by the first.

$20 \div 100 = \frac{1}{5}$ ← Check by dividing the third term by the second.

The common ratio is $\frac{1}{5}$

b) Write the first five terms of the sequence that starts with 4 and has a common ratio of $\sqrt{2}$.

The 1st term is 4

The 2nd term is $4 \times \sqrt{2} = 4\sqrt{2}$

The 3rd term is $4\sqrt{2} \times \sqrt{2} = 4 \times 2 = 8$

The 4th term is $8 \times \sqrt{2} = 8\sqrt{2}$

The 5th term is $8\sqrt{2} \times \sqrt{2} = 16$

## Other special number sequences

Square, cube and triangular numbers are sequences you should be familiar with that do not have a simple term-to-term rule.

The square numbers are the sequence that results from squaring a value.

The cube numbers are the sequence that results from cubing a value.

The triangular numbers are the sequence for which a representation can be made in the shape of an equilateral triangle.

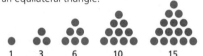

| 1 | 3 | 6 | 10 | 15 |

Make sure you know these square, cube and triangular numbers.

Square: 1, 4, 9, 16, 25, 36, 49, 64, 81, 100, 121, 144 ...

Cube: 1, 8, 27, 64, 125, 216, 343, 512, 729, 1000, ...

Triangular: 1, 3, 6, 10, 15, 21, 28, ...

Work out the next term in the sequence 3, 5, 8, 12, 17, ...

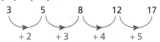

| 3 | 5 | 8 | 12 | 17 |

+2    +3    +4    +5

The sequence is increasing by +2, then +3, then +4, and so on.

The next term is $17 + 6 = 23$

## Fibonacci-style sequences

In the Fibonacci sequence, each term is the sum of the two previous terms.

The Fibonacci sequence starts with 1 and 1.

The 3rd term is $1 + 1 = 2$    The 4th term is $1 + 2 = 3$

The 5th term is $2 + 3 = 5$    The 6th term is $3 + 5 = 8$

And so on.

Work out the next three terms in the Fibonacci-style sequence 3, 4, ...

The 3rd term is: $3 + 4 = 7$

The 4th term is: $4 + 7 = 11$

The 5th term is: $7 + 11 = 18$

# 2 Other types of sequences

## Geometric sequences

**1** Work out the common ratio of each sequence. Then write the missing terms.

**a)** 3, 6, 12, 24, _____, _____

Common ratio: _____

**b)** 81, 27, 9, 3, _____, _____

Common ratio: _____

**c)** 1, –2, 4, –8, _____, _____

Common ratio: _____

**d)** $3\sqrt{3}$, 9, _____, _____, $27\sqrt{3}$

Common ratio: _____

## Other special number sequences

**2** Work out the next **two** terms in each sequence.

**a)** 4, 7, 12, 19, _____, _____

**b)** 20, 10, 2, –4, _____, _____

## Fibonacci-style sequences

**3** Work out the next **three** terms in each of these Fibonacci-style sequences.

**a)** 2, 8, _____, _____, _____

**b)** –2, –4, _____, _____, _____

# (2) Quadratic sequences

## Using the $n$th term rule

Quadratic sequences involve square numbers, so they do not increase or decrease by a constant amount.

Using the $n$th term rule to find a term of a quadratic sequence is the same as using the $n$th term rule for any other sequence.

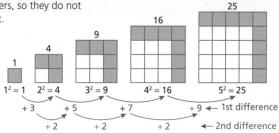

The general form of a quadratic sequence is $u_n = an^2 + bn + c$

| | |
|---|---|
| The $n$th term rule of a sequence is $2n^2 - 3$. | When $n = 1$: $(2 \times 1^2) - 3 = -1$ |
| Work out the first five terms of the sequence. | When $n = 2$: $(2 \times 2^2) - 3 = 5$ |
| | When $n = 3$: $(2 \times 3^2) - 3 = 15$ |
| | When $n = 4$: $(2 \times 4^2) - 3 = 29$ |
| | When $n = 5$: $(2 \times 5^2) - 3 = 47$ |

## Working out the $n$th term rule

In a quadratic sequence, the **second difference** is constant.

**To work out the $n$th term of a quadratic sequence:**
1. Find the second difference between the terms.
2. The coefficient of $n^2$ is half of the second difference.
3. Write out the sequence of $an^2$.
4. Subtract the terms of the original sequence from the sequence of $an^2$.
5. Find the $n$th term rule of the resulting linear sequence.
6. Combine the $n$th term rule for the linear sequence with $an^2$ to find the $n$th term rule for the quadratic sequence.

Work out the $n$th term rule of the sequence 1, 12, 29, 52, ...

The second difference is 6, so $a = 3$.

A table can be helpful to organise your working but isn't necessary.

| **Given sequence:** | 1 | 12 | 29 | 52 |
|---|---|---|---|---|
| $an^2$ **sequence:** | 3 | 12 | 27 | 48 |
| **Difference:** | −2 | 0 | 2 | 4 |

Subtract the $3n^2$ sequence from the given sequence. Write down a sequence of $3n^2$. $+2 \quad +2 \quad +2$

Find the $n$th term rule for the sequence −2, 0, 2, 4, ...

The sequence is linked to the 2 times table so the $n$th term will be of the form $2n + c$.

When $n = 1$: $(2 \times 1) + c = -2 \Rightarrow c = -4$

The $n$th term rule of this linear sequence is $2n - 4$.

Combine the $n$th term rule for the linear sequence with $an^2$.

The $n$th term rule of the given quadratic sequence is $3n^2 + 2n - 4$.

Work out the $n$th term rule of the sequence 3, 9, 19, 33, ...

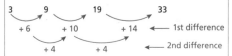

The second difference is 4, so $a = 4 \div 2 = 2$.
The sequence $2n^2$ is 2, 8, 18, 32.
The $n$th term rule is $2n^2 + 1$.

## 2 Quadratic sequences

## Using the $n$th term rule

**1** Work out the first five terms of each sequence.

**a)** $n^2 + 4n$

**b)** $2n^2 + 3n - 1$

## Working out the $n$th term rule

**2** Work out the $n$th term rule of the sequence 2, 8, 16, 26, 38, …

**3** Work out the $n$th term rule of the sequence −2, −1, 4, 13, 26, …

**4** Work out the $n$th term rule of the sequence 4, 15, 34, 61, 96, …

# 3 Converting units

## Converting units of length, area and volume

Units of length are mm, cm, m, km, and so on.
Units of area are units of length squared, e.g. $mm^2$, $cm^2$, $m^2$, and so on.
Units of volume are units of length cubed, e.g. $mm^3$, $cm^3$, $m^3$, and so on. Units of volume can also be given in ml, cl, l, and so on. In this case, convert between them in the same way as you do for lengths.

To convert between units of length:

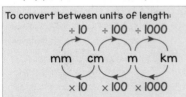

$\div 10 \quad \div 100 \quad \div 1000$

mm cm m km

$\times 10 \quad \times 100 \quad \times 1000$

A solar panel is 320 cm wide.
How wide is it in metres?

There are 100 cm in 1 m.

$320 \div 100 = 3.2$

The solar panel is 3.2 m wide.

To convert between units of area:

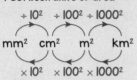

$\div 10^2 \quad \div 100^2 \quad \div 1000^2$

$mm^2 \quad cm^2 \quad m^2 \quad km^2$

$\times 10^2 \quad \times 100^2 \quad \times 1000^2$

A table has an area of $1.5\,m^2$.
What is its area in centimetres squared?

There are 100 cm in 1 m so multiply by $100^2$.

$1.5 \times 100^2 = 1.5 \times 10\,000 = 15\,000$

The table has an area of $15\,000\,cm^2$.

To convert between units of volume:

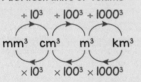

$\div 10^3 \quad \div 100^3 \quad \div 1000^3$

$mm^3 \quad cm^3 \quad m^3 \quad km^3$

$\times 10^3 \quad \times 100^3 \quad \times 1000^3$

A metal drum holds 400 l of oil.
How many cubic metres does it hold?

There are 1000 ml in 1 litre.

$400\,l = 400\,000\,ml$

$400\,000\,ml = 400\,000\,cm^3$ ← $1\,ml = 1\,cm^3$

$400\,000\,cm^3 \div 100^3 = 0.4\,m^3$

## Area and volume of similar shapes

Similar shapes are shapes that have corresponding sides in the same ratio. You can use the same idea of converting units when working out areas and volumes of similar shapes.

For similar shapes with lengths in the ratio of $1 : n$, the ratio of the areas is $1 : n^2$.
For similar solids with lengths in the ratio of $1 : n$, the ratio of the volumes is $1 : n^3$.

These rectangles are similar with a scale factor of 2.

Work out the area of the larger rectangle.

The area of the smaller rectangle is
$3\,cm \times 5\,cm = 15\,cm^2$

The area of the larger rectangle is
$15 \times 2^2 = 60\,cm^2$ ← Multiply by the scale factor squared.

These cuboids are similar with a scale factor of $\frac{1}{2}$.

Calculate the volume of the smaller cuboid.

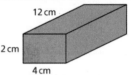

Volume of the larger cuboid $= 2\,cm \times 4\,cm \times 12\,cm$
$= 96\,cm^3$

Volume of the smaller cuboid $= 96 \times \left(\frac{1}{2}\right)^3$
$= 96 \div 8 = 12\,cm^3$

#  Converting units

## Converting units of length, area and volume

**1** A pentagonal prism has a surface area of 20.14 cm².

Work out its surface area in millimetres squared.

................................ mm²

**2** The prism in question 1 has a volume of 6.45 cm³.

Work out its volume in cubic metres, giving your answer in standard form.

................................ m³

## Area and volume of similar shapes

**3** A coffee shop sells keychains with scale models of its coffee cups.

Actual coffee cup:                    Model coffee cup:

                     5.5 cm

16.5 cm

The volume of the actual coffee cup is 354 cm³.

What is the volume of the model coffee cup? Give your answer to the nearest cubic centimetre.

................................ cm³

**4** Here are two similar rectangles, A and B.

**A**                **B**

Area = 30 m²        Area = 120 m²

Work out the linear scale factor of enlargement from rectangle A to B.

................................

# ③ Scale factors

## Scale factors in shapes

A **scale factor** is a ratio between corresponding measurements that shows how much a length has been enlarged.

Line CD is three times the length of AB. The scale factor from line AB to line CD is 3.

A———2 cm———B

C————————6 cm————————D

> In an enlarged shape, each side is multiplied by the same scale factor.

a)   Shape B is an enlargement of shape A. Work out the scale factor.

Diagrams not drawn to scale

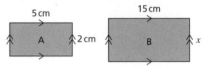

15 cm ÷ 5 cm = 3, so the scale factor is 3.

b)   Work out the side length $x$.

$3 \times 2\,\text{cm} = 6\,\text{cm}$

## Scale diagrams

**To use a scale factor on a diagram:**
1.   Measure the desired length.
2.   Multiply by the scale factor to find the actual length.

> Make sure you multiply by the scale factor.

The scale drawing below shows a plan for a large garden with a grassy area and a patio.

a)   Calculate the area of the section where grass will be planted.

> Split the grassy section into a square and a triangle.

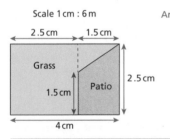

> The scale is 1 cm = 6 m, so multiply each measurement by 6 to find the actual lengths.

$\text{Area} = 15\,\text{m} \times 15\,\text{m}$
$= 225\,\text{m}^2$

$2.5 \times 6 = 15\,\text{m}$   $1.5 \times 6 = 9\,\text{m}$

$\text{Area} = \frac{1}{2} \times 6\,\text{m} \times 9\,\text{m}$
$= 27\,\text{m}^2$

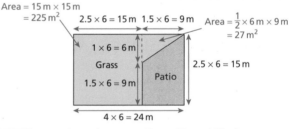

Area of square = $15\,\text{m} \times 15\,\text{m} = 225\,\text{m}^2$
Area of triangle = $\frac{1}{2} \times 6\,\text{m} \times 9\,\text{m} = 27\,\text{m}^2$
Total area = $252\,\text{m}^2$

b)   Grass seed is sold in bags of 5 kg, 10 kg and 20 kg.
A 5 kg bag will cover an area of 100 m² and costs £38.50
A 10 kg bag will cover an area of 200 m² and costs £60.50
A 20 kg bag will cover an area of 400 m² costs and £108.50
What is the cheapest way of buying enough seed to cover the grassy area and what is the cost?

> Work out possible combinations of bags to cover the area needed.

Three 5 kg bags will cover 300 m² and cost £38.50 × 3 = £115.50
One 5 kg bag and one 10 kg bag will cover 300 m² and cost £38.50 + £60.50 = £99
One 20 kg bag covers 400 m² costs and £108.50
The cheapest option is one 5 kg bag and one 10 kg bag. Total cost £99.

# ③ Scale factors

## Scale factors in shapes

**1** Shape B is an enlargement of shape A.

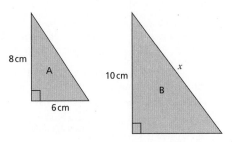

Work out the length of the side labelled $x$. ............................... cm

## Scale diagrams

**2** Here is a diagram of a lounge drawn to a scale of 2 units : 1 m.

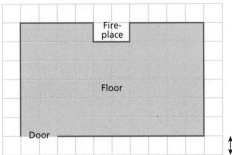

**a)** Calculate the actual area of the floor in the lounge.

............................... m²

**b)** Carpet is sold in rolls of 4 m width in any length needed at a price of £13.99 per square metre. How much will it cost to cover the floor with carpet?

£ ...............................

# ③ Ratio

## Simplifying ratios

A **ratio** is used to compare two or more quantities and is written with a colon ( : ) between each value, e.g. the ratio of red to blue beads is 5 : 3.

To simplify a ratio means to write the ratio so that there are no common factors between the values.

> To simplify a ratio, divide all the parts by the same number until they cannot be divided any further.

> The scale on a map is given as 1 cm to 2 km. Express this as a ratio in its simplest form.
>
> 1 km = 1000 metres; 1 metre = 100 cm
>
> So 2 km = 200 000 cm ← Change to a common unit.
>
> The ratio of the map is
>
> 1 cm : 200 000 cm
>
> = 1 : 200 000 ← Cancel out the units.

Express 30 cm to 2 metres as a ratio in its simplest form.

30 cm : 2 metres = 30 cm : 200 cm

= 3 : 20 | When working with ratios, always use common units so they can cancel out.

## Unit ratios

A **unit ratio** is written in the form 1 : $n$ or $n$ : 1. It can be used to compare ratios.

a) The ratio of cupcakes to biscuits at a party is 2 : 3. Write the ratio in the form 1 : $n$.

÷ 2 ⟋ 2 : 3 ⟍ ÷ 2
    ⟍ 1 : 1.5 ⟋

2 ÷ 2 = 1, so divide both sides by 2. This unit ratio means that for every one cupcake at the party, there are 1.5 biscuits.

b) At a small school, there are 173 students and 7 teachers. At a larger school, there are 550 students and 23 teachers. Which school has more students per teacher?

Write each ratio students : teacher in the form $n$ : 1.

They are now both in the form $n$ : 1 so you can compare them.

÷ 7 ⟋ 173 : 7 ⟍ ÷ 7      ÷ 23 ⟋ 550 : 23 ⟍ ÷ 23
    ⟍ 24.71 : 1 ⟋              ⟍ 23.91 : 1 ⟋

24.71 > 23.91, so the ratio of students to teachers is greater in the smaller school.

The smaller school has a larger number of students per teacher.

## Ratios with decimals and fractions

Ratios can be written with decimals or fractions.

**To simplify a ratio with a decimal:**
1. Multiply all parts by the same value to make them integers.
2. Divide by the highest common factor.

> To simplify a ratio with a decimal or a fraction, first convert all the parts into integers.

**To simplify a ratio with a fraction:**
1. Write the fractions with a common denominator.
2. Multiply all the fractions by the common denominator.
3. Divide by the highest common factor.

Simplify 1.4 : 5

1.4 : 5 | Multiply both parts of the ratio by 10 so that you are working with integers.

= 14 : 50

= 7 : 25 ← Simplify by dividing both sides by 2.

Simplify $\frac{2}{3} : \frac{3}{4}$

$\frac{2}{3} = \frac{8}{12}$ and $\frac{3}{4} = \frac{9}{12}$ ← Write both fractions with a common denominator.

$\frac{8}{12} : \frac{9}{12}$

= 8 : 9 ← Multiply by the denominator.

# Ratio

## Simplifying ratios

**1** Write each ratio in simplest form.

**a)** 3 : 12

**b)** 4 : 10

**c)** 2 cm : 1 km

**d)** 15 kg : 800 g

## Unit ratios

**2** Sara buys two bottles of squash which are both mixed with water to make a drink.
Bottle A requires 500 ml of squash and 1500 ml of water to make 2 litres of the drink.
Bottle B requires 160 ml of squash and 640 ml of water to make 800 ml of the drink.

**a)** Write the ratio of squash to water in each drink in the form $n$ : 1.

Bottle A ............................

Bottle B ............................

**b)** Which bottle of squash requires a higher amount of squash per millilitre of water?

## Ratios with decimals and fractions

**3** Simplify the ratios.

**a)** 15 : 0.5

**b)** $\frac{2}{5} : \frac{4}{7}$

#  Further ratio

## Dividing a quantity into a given ratio

You can share quantities into a given ratio. The parts in the ratio represent the proportions.

A drink is made of orange juice and water in the ratio 1 : 4.

How much water is used in a 200 ml drink?

1 + 4 = 5 parts in the ratio.

200 ml ÷ 5 = 40 ml ← Divide 200 ml by 5 parts to find the amount in 1 part of the ratio.

40 ml × 4 = 160 ml

160 ml of water in a 200 ml drink. ← Multiply to find the value of 4 parts in the ratio.

**To divide into a given ratio:**

1. Count the total parts of the ratio.
2. Divide the quantity by the total parts to find the value of one part.
3. Multiply by each part.

A paint is made by mixing blue, red and white paint in the ratio 3 : 2 : 2. A decorator needs 2.1 litres of paint. How much blue, red and white paint do they need?

3 + 2 + 2 = 7 parts in the ratio

2.1 litres = 2100 ml and

2100 ml ÷ 7 = 300 ml ← Divide 2.1 litres by 7 to find the amount in 1 part of the ratio.

Three parts is 300 ml × 3 = 900 ml

Two parts is 300 ml × 2 = 600 ml

The decorator needs 900 ml of blue, 600 ml of red and 600 ml of white paint.

## Working out missing amounts in a ratio

You can find missing amounts in a ratio given the whole and part of the ratio.

**To work out a missing amount in a ratio:**

1. Divide the given amount by the given number of parts to find the value of one part.
2. Multiply the part corresponding to the unknown value by the result of step 1.

The ratio of adults to children at a football match is 7 : 3. There are 1500 children at the match. How many more adults are there than children?

There are 1500 children, so 3 parts = 1500

1 part = 500 ← Divide both sides by 3.

Adults represent 4 more parts than children.

1 part = 500, so 4 parts = 2000

There are 2000 more adults than children.

Currency exchange is a common context for ratio questions and in real life.

Given an exchange rate of £1 = another currency:
- To change from £ to the other currency, multiply by the exchange rate.
- To change from the other currency to £, divide by the exchange rate.

Meena is on holiday in France. The exchange rate is £1 = €1.16

She buys a meal for €70. How much does she spend in £?

€1.16 = £1

€70 = 70 ÷ 1.16 ← Divide by the exchange rate.

= £60.34

## Ratios as fractions

Matthew and Natasha share a pizza in the ratio 3 : 2. What fraction does Matthew eat?

Use the total number of parts in the ratio to represent the total number of pieces of pizza. Then write the number Matthew eats as a fraction of the total number of pieces.

The ratio has 5 parts altogether.

Matthew eats 3 out of the 5 parts, so he eats $\frac{3}{5}$ of the pizza.

When writing a ratio as a fraction, the denominator is the total number of parts in the ratio.

# ③ Further ratio

## Dividing a quantity into a given ratio

1. Gary is raising money for charity. He will donate to charity X and charity Y in the ratio 2 : 3. He raises £1200.

How much does each charity receive?

Charity X = £ .....................

Charity Y = £ .....................

## Working out missing amounts in a ratio

2. Katya is also raising money for charity. She donates to three charities (A, B and C) in the ratio 1 : 3 : 2. She donates £54 to charity B.

**a)** How much does she donate to charity A and charity C?

Charity A = £ .....................

Charity C = £ .....................

**b)** How much does she donate in total?

£ .....................

## Ratios as fractions

3. The ratio of adults to children at a cinema is 4 : 1.

**a)** Write the proportion of adults as a fraction of all the people at the cinema.

.....................

**b)** There are 120 people at the cinema.

How many of them are adults?

.....................

# ③ Proportion

## Proportion calculations

A **proportion** is a comparison of a part to a whole. Two values are in **direct proportion** if the ratio between them remains fixed as the values change, e.g. the number of miles travelled when driving at a constant speed.

You can use the **unitary method** or **equivalence method** to solve problems in direct proportion.

**To use the unitary method**:
1. Write out the proportion.
2. Find the amount of one part of the whole.
3. Multiply to find the desired amount.

The unitary method works by finding the value of one unit. If the numbers work out nicely, the equivalence method may be easier.

**To use the equivalence method**:
1. Write out the proportion.
2. Write out the proportion you are trying to find.
3. Work out the multiplier (divide the bottom by the top).
4. Multiply the other side by the multiplier.

a) Here are some ingredients needed to make 12 biscuits:

Work out the amount of sugar needed to make 18 biscuits.

100 g butter
60 g sugar
120 g flour

**Unitary method**

$\div 12$ ⟋ 60 g = 12 biscuits ⟍ $\div 12$
      5 g = 1 biscuit
$\times 18$ ⟍ 90 g = 18 biscuits ⟋ $\times 18$

**Equivalence method**

60 g = 12 biscuits
___ g = 18 biscuits ← The proportion you are trying to find.

18 ÷ 12 = 1.5, so the multiplier is 1.5

$\times 1.5$ ⟋ 60 g = 12 biscuits ⟍ $\times 1.5$
    90 g = 18 biscuits

b) Two bags of flour cost £2.36. How much do three bags cost?

$\div 2$ ⟋ 2 bags = £2.36 ⟍ $\div 2$
   1 bag = £1.18
$\times 3$ ⟍ 3 bags = £3.54 ⟋ $\times 3$

## Value for money

A common application of proportions is working out the best value for money, or the best deal.

To compare value for money, work out the cost per unit or use the equivalence method.

A bottle of laundry detergent costs £9.00 for 50 washes.
A box of laundry capsules is on offer for £5.00 for 30 washes.
Which is the better deal?

**Comparing the cost per wash**

Bottle of detergent:

Divide by 50 to find the cost of one wash.

$\div 50$ ⟋ £9.00 = 50 washes ⟍ $\div 50$
   18p = 1 wash

Alternatively, you could work out how much 30 washes would cost using the bottle of detergent or how much 50 washes would cost using the box of capsules.

Laundry capsules:

$\div 30$ ⟋ £5.00 = 30 washes ⟍ $\div 30$
   16.67p = 1 wash

The laundry capsules are a better deal as they cost less per wash.

# 3 Proportion

## Proportion calculations

**1** A recipe is shown for Yorkshire pudding to serve 4 people.

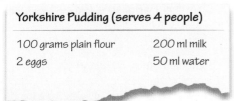

**Yorkshire Pudding (serves 4 people)**

100 grams plain flour       200 ml milk

2 eggs                      50 ml water

How much of each ingredient is needed to make Yorkshire pudding for 6 people?

**a)** Flour

**b)** Milk

........................ g

........................ ml

**c)** Eggs

**d)** Water

........................

........................ ml

## Value for money

**2** A 700 g bag of carrots costs £0.90
A 500 g bag of carrots costs £0.50

Which is the better deal? Show your workings.

........................

**3** A 200 ml bottle of shampoo costs £4.50
A 500 ml bottle of shampoo costs £8.00

Which is the better deal? Show your workings.

........................

# Percentages

## Calculating and writing percentages

A **percentage** (%) is a fraction of an amount, meaning the amount per hundred.

**To calculate a percentage of a quantity, either:**
- convert the percentage to a fraction or a decimal and multiply        *or*
- break down the percentage into tens and ones and combine as needed.

> To find 10% of a quantity, divide the quantity by 10.
> To find 5% of a quantity, divide 10% of the quantity by 2.
> To find 1% of a quantity, divide the quantity by 100.

To write one quantity as a percentage of another, make sure both quantities are in the same units then express the quantity as a fraction of the other and convert to a percentage.

---

Work out 82% of 200 grams.

**Method 1 (calculator)**

82% is $\frac{82}{100}$

$\frac{82}{100} \times 200\,g = 164\,g$

**Method 2 (non-calculator)**

10% of 200g is $200 \div 10 = 20$

1% of 200g is $200 \div 100 = 2$    80% is 10% × 8

Then 80% of 200g is $20 \times 8 = 160$

And 2% of 200g is $2 \times 2 = 4$    2% is 1% × 2

So 82% of 200g is $160 + 4 = 164\,g$.

---

Express 50p as a percentage of £2.

$\frac{50}{200} = \frac{25}{100} = 25\%$    £2 = 200p. Write 50p as a fraction of 200p and simplify.

## Percentage change

**To work out the percentage change:**
1. Work out the change, e.g. increase, decrease, profit or loss.
2. Use the formula
   percentage change = $\frac{\text{change}}{\text{original amount}} \times 100\%$

**To increase or decrease a quantity by a percentage:**
1. Work out the increase or decrease.
2. Add the increase to the original amount (or subtract the decrease).

**Or**
1. Write down the multiplier.
2. Multiply the original amount by the multiplier.

> Using multipliers is the quickest way to work out repeated percentage change.

---

Mr Smith bought a ring for £250 and sold it for £400. Work out his percentage profit.

percentage profit = $\frac{\text{profit}}{\text{original amount}} \times 100\%$

£400 – £250 is £150 profit.    $= \frac{150}{250} \times 100\% = 60\%$

---

Increase £17 000 by 5%.

**Method 1**

5% of £17 000 is $\frac{5}{100} \times 17\,000 = £850$

New amount is £17 000 + £850 = £17 850

**Method 2 (multiplier method)**

5% extra is the same as 100% + 5% = 105%

105% is $\frac{105}{100} = 1.05$    The decimal equivalent is called the multiplier.

105% of £17 000 is $1.05 \times 17\,000 = £17\,850$

## Working out the original amount

**To work out the original amount:**
1. Write down the multiplier.
2. Divide the final amount by the multiplier.

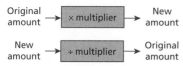

---

A car is worth £12 300 after losing 18% of its value in one year. What was its value one year ago?    The car loses value so subtract the percentage from 100.

100% – 18% = 82%

82% = 0.82    0.82 is the multiplier.

£12 300 ÷ 0.82 = £15 000

# Percentages

## Calculating and writing percentages

**1** Without using a calculator, work out 32% of 640 grams.

.................................. g

**2** What is 265 m as a percentage of 26.5 km?

.................................. %

## Percentage change

**3** A shirt has been reduced in price from £15 to £12.

What is the percentage reduction of the price of the shirt?

.................................. %

**4** Kerry opens a bank account with £1200. The account pays 3% simple interest per year.

Work out the amount in her account after one year.

£ ..................................

## Working out the original amount

**5** A builder charges £3000 for a job, including 20% VAT.

What is the cost of the job before VAT?

£ ..................................

# 3 Direct and inverse proportion

## Direct proportion

Two values are in **direct proportion** if the ratio between each pair of values is the same. For example, the amount of a sugar in a recipe has to double in order to make double the number of biscuits.

Direct proportion can be expressed as an equation, $y = kx$, where k is the **constant of proportionality**.

The graph of direct proportion is a straight line starting at the origin with a gradient of k.

This is the graph of $y = 2x$. The gradient is $k = 2$, so every $y$ value is twice the corresponding $x$ value.

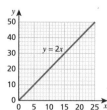

**To set up an equation of proportionality:**

1. Write the proportion using the symbol $\propto$
2. Write the proportion as an equation in terms of k.
3. Substitute the values given in the problem to find the value of k.
4. Rewrite the equation substituting in the value of k.

$y$ can also be proportional to $x^2$, $x^3$, $\sqrt{x}$, and so on. In this case, the equation becomes $y = kx^2$, $y = kx^3$, $y = k\sqrt{x}$, etc.

> Proportionality can be shown using the symbol $\propto$, where $y \propto x$ means 'y is proportional to x'.

---

$y$ is directly proportional to $x$.
When $y = 21$, $x = 7$.

**Work out the value of $y$ when $x = 2$.**

$y \propto x$ ← Write the proportional relationship.

$y = kx$ ← Write the equation in terms of k.

$21 = 7k$ ← Substitute the values of $x = 7$ and $y = 21$.

$3 = k$ ← This is the constant of proportionality.

$y = 3k$ ← This is the equation of proportionality.

$y = 3 \times 2$ ← Substitute $x = 2$.

$y = 6$

---

$y$ is proportional to the square of $x$.
When $y = 18$, $x = 3$.

**Work out the value of $y$ when $x = 5$.**

$y \propto x^2$ ← Write the proportional relationship.

$y = kx^2$ ← Write the equation in terms of k.

$18 = k \times 3^2$ ← Substitute $x = 3$ and $y = 18$.

$18 = 9k \Rightarrow$ then $k = 2$

So $y = 2x^2$ ← This is the equation of proportionality.

When $x = 5$, $y = 2 \times 5^2 = 50$

## Inverse proportion

Two values are **inversely proportional** if as one value increases, the other decreases at the same rate, e.g. as one doubles, the other halves.

> If two quantities $y$ and $x$ are inversely proportional, we write $y \propto \frac{1}{x}$ or $y = \frac{k}{x}$

$y$ can also be inversely proportional to $x^2$, $x^3$, $\sqrt{x}$, and so on.

A graph of inverse proportion is a **reciprocal** curve.

For all inverse proportion graphs, as $x$ gets bigger, $y$ gets smaller.

$y$ is inversely proportional to the cube root of $x$. When $y = 2$, $x = 8$.

**Work out the value of $y$ when $x = 27$.**

$y \propto \frac{1}{\sqrt[3]{x}}$ or $y = \frac{k}{\sqrt[3]{x}}$

$y = 2$, $x = 8$, so $2 = \frac{k}{\sqrt[3]{8}}$ giving $k = 4$

So $y = \frac{4}{\sqrt[3]{x}}$

When $x = 27$, $y = \frac{4}{\sqrt[3]{27}} = \frac{4}{3}$

# Direct and inverse proportion

## Direct proportion

**1** $y$ is directly proportional to $x$. When $y = 9$, $x = 3$.

Work out the value of $y$ when $x = 4$.

$y = $ ...............................

**2** $y$ is directly proportional to $\sqrt{x}$. When $y = 16$, $x = 4$.

Work out the value of $y$ when $x = 25$.

$y = $ ...............................

## Inverse proportion

**3** $y$ is inversely proportional to $x$. When $y = 3$, $x = 6$.

Work out the value of $y$ when $x = 4$.

$y = $ ...............................

**4** $y$ is inversely proportional to $x^2$. When $y = 4$, $x = 3$.

Work out the value of $y$ when $x = 2$.

$y = $ ...............................

**5** A printer has enough ink to last 3 weeks when it prints 600 pages a day.

How long will the ink last if 200 pages a day are printed?

...............................

# ③ Compound units

## Speed

A **compound measure** or **compound unit** is a measure of one quantity in relation to another. Speed is an example of a compound measure.

**Speed** is the distance travelled divided by the time taken. The units for speed are a distance (e.g. metres, kilometres, miles) per a unit of time (e.g. hours, minutes, seconds).

You can draw a formula triangle to help remember related formulae for compound measures.

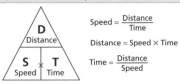

$$\text{Speed} = \frac{\text{Distance}}{\text{Time}}$$

$$\text{Distance} = \text{Speed} \times \text{Time}$$

$$\text{Time} = \frac{\text{Distance}}{\text{Speed}}$$

A cyclist completes a 231 km road race at an average speed of 44 km/h. What was their race time? Give your answer in hours and minutes.

Time = Distance ÷ Speed ◄──── Use the formula triangle.

Time = 231 ÷ 44 = 5.25 = 5 hours and 15 minutes ◄──── 0.25 hours = 60 × 0.25 = 15 minutes

## Density and pressure

**Density** is a measure of a material's mass divided by its volume. The units are a measure of mass per unit of volume (e.g. $g/cm^3$).

**Pressure** is a measure of a force divided by the area to which the force is applied. The units are a measure of force per unit of area (e.g. $N/m^2$, where N is a Newton, a measure of force).

$$\text{Pressure} = \frac{\text{Force}}{\text{Area}}$$

$$\text{Force} = \text{Pressure} \times \text{Area}$$

$$\text{Area} = \frac{\text{Force}}{\text{Pressure}}$$

$$\text{Density} = \frac{\text{Mass}}{\text{Volume}}$$

$$\text{Mass} = \text{Density} \times \text{Volume}$$

$$\text{Volume} = \frac{\text{Mass}}{\text{Density}}$$

Ohm's law states that $V = I \times R$ where $V$ = voltage in volts (V), $I$ = current in amperes (A) and $R$ = resistance in ohms (Ω). Work out the current when the resistance is 115 Ω and the voltage is 230 V.

Draw a formula triangle knowing that $I \times R$ will go on the bottom and $V$ will go on the top.

$$I = V \div R$$

$$I = 230\,V \div 115\,Ω = 2\,A$$

The air pressure inside a tyre is $220\,000\,N/m^2$. The area of tyre that touches the road is $0.005\,m^2$. Work out the force applied by the tyre on the road.

Force = Pressure × Area ◄── Use the formula triangle.

Force = $220\,000\,N/m^2 \times 0.005\,m^2$

Force = 1100 N

## Rates

A rate is a compound measure: something happens in a unit of time (e.g. the rate of water filling up a pool).

a) A hosepipe flows at a rate of 12 litres per minute as it fills up a 420-litre paddling pool. How long does it take to fill the pool?

Draw a formula triangle. The rate is the volume per minute.

Time = Volume ÷ Rate

Time = 420 l ÷ 12 l/min = 35 minutes

b) Petrol flows from a pump at a rate of 13 litres per minute. The pump takes 3 minutes to fill a petrol tank.

What is the volume of the tank?

Volume = Rate × Time

Volume = 13 l/min × 3 min = 39 litres

# Compound units

## Speed

**1** A car travels a distance of 140 km at an average speed of 40 km/h.

How long does the journey take?

.................................... h

**2** An aeroplane departs at 11:05 and lands at 13:15. It flies at an average speed of 924 km/h.

How far has the aeroplane flown?

.................................... km

## Density and pressure

**3** Gold has a density of approximately 19 g/cm³.

What is the volume of a gold bar of mass 11 kg? Give your answer to the nearest cubic centimetre.

.................................... cm³

**4** A kettlebell exerts a force of 60 N on the floor over an area of 0.012 m².

Calculate the pressure exerted by the kettlebell on the floor.

$$\text{Pressure} = \frac{\text{Force}}{\text{Area}}$$

.................................... N/m²

## Rates

**5** Sand falls through a three-minute egg timer at a rate of 0.6 g/s.

What is the mass of sand in the timer?

.................................... g

# ③ Rates of change

## Writing and interpreting rates of change in equations

A **rate of change** is a measure of how one value changes in relation to another.

> A straight line has a constant rate of change. A horizontal line means there is no change.

Write an equation to represent each scenario.

a) Car hire costs £40 per day. Write an equation showing the total cost for hiring a car for $d$ days.

> It can help to write the equation in words.

Total cost = £40 × number of days

$T = 40d$ where $T$ is the total cost and $d$ is the number of days.

> Remember to say what the variables are.

b) A gardener charges £30 an hour plus a fixed travel cost of £20. Write an equation showing the total cost to hire the gardener for $h$ hours.

> The £20 travel cost is constant; it is the same whatever the number of hours worked.

Total cost = (£30 × number of hours) + £20

$T = 30h + 20$ where $T$ is the total cost and $h$ is the number of hours.

## Interpreting rates of change on graphs

On a straight-line graph, the gradient is the rate of change and the $y$-intercept is the initial value.

On a curved graph, the rate of change is **not** constant and is represented by the gradient at a particular point (see page 42).

The graph shows the total cost of hiring a pressure washer, including the delivery fee.

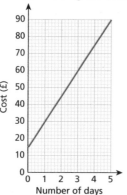

*Cost (£) vs Number of days*

a) Write down the delivery fee.

The delivery fee is the $y$-intercept, £15.

b) Work out the cost per day to hire the pressure washer.

Gradient = $\dfrac{\text{change in } y}{\text{change in } x} = \dfrac{90 - 15}{5 - 0} = 15$

> (0, 15) and (5, 90) are two convenient points for working out the change in $y$ in relation to $x$.

It is £15 per day to hire the pressure washer.

Rates of change can be compared by looking at the steepness of the lines.

Ice is heated until it boils as water. The graph shows its temperature change.

At what rate does the temperature of the water increase from the ice melting to boiling point?

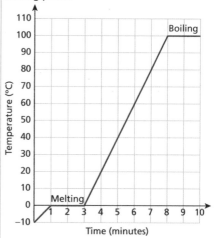

*Temperature (°C) vs Time (minutes)*

At melting point (0°C), the water begins to heat up at (3, 0). It begins to boil at (8, 100).

Gradient = $\dfrac{\text{change in } y}{\text{change in } x} = \dfrac{100 - 0}{8 - 3} = \dfrac{100}{5} = 20$

The temperature of the water increases by 20°C per minute.

> The steeper the straight line, the greater the rate of change.

# 3 ) Rates of change

## Writing and interpreting rates of change in equations

**1** Write equations to model each situation.

**a)** The number of steps taken when walking. Jai takes 2000 steps per mile when walking.

.................................................................................................................................

.................................................................................................................................

**b)** The value of a mobile phone that costs £500 when new. It decreases in value by £50 per year.

.................................................................................................................................

.................................................................................................................................

**c)** The total volume of water in a swimming pool being filled with a hosepipe that flows at 12 litres per minute.

.................................................................................................................................

.................................................................................................................................

## Interpreting rates of change on graphs

**2** The graph shows Paul's drive from home to work.

He stops at a coffee shop on the way.

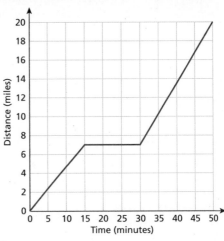

**a)** How far is the coffee shop from Paul's house?

................................ miles

**b)** Does he drive faster from home to the coffee shop or from the coffee shop to work? Explain your answer.

.................................................................................................................................

.................................................................................................................................

**c)** How fast does Paul drive to work from the coffee shop?

................................ mph

# 3 Exponential growth and decay

## Compound interest and exponential growth

**Simple interest** means that the initial amount earns interest. **Compound interest** means the interest is earned on the balance in the account, including any previous interest earned.

Compound interest is an example of **exponential growth** because there is repeated percentage change. It is best calculated using a multiplier.

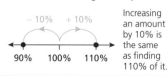

Decreasing an amount by 10% is the same as finding 90% of it.

Increasing an amount by 10% is the same as finding 110% of it.

To increase an amount by $r\%$, multiply by $1 + \frac{r}{100}$

To decrease an amount by $r\%$, multiply by $1 - \frac{r}{100}$

$A = P\left(1 + \frac{r}{100}\right)^n$ where $A$ is the amount after $n$ increases, $P$ is the initial amount, $r$ is the rate of change and $n$ is the number of increases.

**To work out values of repeated percentage change:**
1. Find the multiplier.
2. Substitute the given values into the formula (above) and work out the value needed.

---

£2000 is invested at 5% compound interest. Work out the value of the investment after 5 years.

**Using a table**

| No. of years | Amount in account |
|---|---|
| 0 | £2000 |
| 1 | £2000 × 1.05 = £2100 |
| 2 | £2100 × 1.05 = £2205 |
| 3 | £2205 × 1.05 = £2315.25 |
| 4 | £2315.25 × 1.05 = £2431.01 |
| 5 | £2431.01 × 1.05 = £2552.56 |

**Using the formula**

$A = P\left(1 + \frac{r}{100}\right)^n$    $P = £2000$, $r = 0.05$ and $n = 5$.

$= 2000 \times 1.05^5 = £2552.56$

---

An ecologist estimates that a tiger population is increasing by 7% a year due to conservation efforts.

a) If there are currently 175 tigers, estimate the tiger population after 5 years.

$7\% = 0.07$, then $1 + 0.07 = 1.07$

$A = P\left(1 + \frac{r}{100}\right)^n$    The population is increasing.

$A = 175 \times 1.07^5$

$A = 245$ tigers    $P = 175$ and $n = 5$.

b) If the ecologist's estimate holds true, after how many years will the tiger population double?    Use trial and improvement.

$175 \times 2 = 350$

After 10 years, there will be $175 \times 1.07^{10} = 344$ tigers

After 11 years, there will be $175 \times 1.07^{11} = 368$ tigers

After 11 years, there will be more than double.

## Exponential decay

**Exponential decay** occurs when a value decreases by a repeated percentage change.

The battery health of a mobile phone is said to decrease by 4% every 100 charge cycles.

a) Calculate the battery health of a phone that has been through 500 charge cycles.

$A = P\left(1 - \frac{r}{100}\right)^n$    The amount is decreasing.

The 4% loss is for every 100 charges, so $n = 5$ represents 500 charges.

The initial amount is 100% battery health, so $P = 100\%$

$A = 100 \times 0.96^5 = 81.537... = 82\%$ (to nearest %)

$r = 0.04$, so the multiplier is $1 - 0.04 = 0.96$

b) After how many charge cycles will the battery health be less than 75%?

After 600 charge cycles, the health will be $100 \times 0.96^6 = 78.27...\%$

After 700, it will be $100 \times 0.96^7 = 75.14...\%$

After 800, it will be $100 \times 0.96^8 = 72.13...\%$

After 800 charge cycles, it is less than 75%.

# Exponential growth and decay

## Compound interest and exponential growth

**1** £1500 is invested in a savings account that pays 3% compound interest.

Work out the amount in the account after 5 years.

£ ...............................................

**2** There are 25 foxes in a park. The population of foxes increases by 12% a year.

**a)** Calculate the expected number of foxes in the park after 3 years.

...............................................

**b)** How many years will it take for the population to double in number?

...............................................

## Exponential decay

**3** A new computer costs £1200 and loses 16% of its value each year.

Calculate the value of the computer after 4 years.

£ ...............................................

# 4 Constructions (1)

## Constructing triangles

A construction is an accurate drawing made using a combination of a ruler, protractor and a pair of compasses.

> Leave all your construction marks and arcs in place. Don't rub them out.

You can **construct** a triangle if you know any of this information:

- the length of the three sides (SSS)
- the length of two sides and an angle between them (SAS)
- the size of two angles and a side between them (ASA).

> Remember SSS, SAS and ASA to construct triangles. These are the same criteria for congruent triangles.

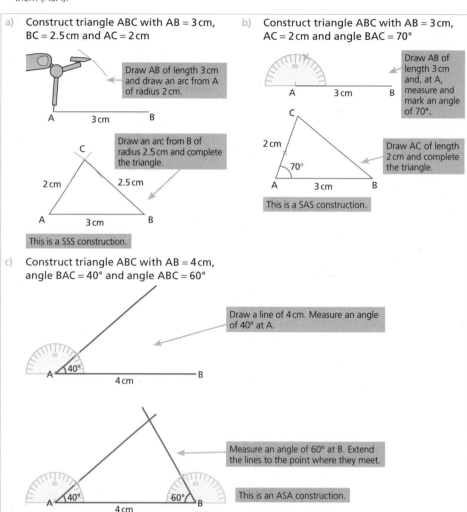

a) Construct triangle ABC with AB = 3 cm, BC = 2.5 cm and AC = 2 cm

Draw AB of length 3 cm and draw an arc from A of radius 2 cm.

Draw an arc from B of radius 2.5 cm and complete the triangle.

This is a SSS construction.

b) Construct triangle ABC with AB = 3 cm, AC = 2 cm and angle BAC = 70°

Draw AB of length 3 cm and, at A, measure and mark an angle of 70°.

Draw AC of length 2 cm and complete the triangle.

This is a SAS construction.

c) Construct triangle ABC with AB = 4 cm, angle BAC = 40° and angle ABC = 60°

Draw a line of 4 cm. Measure an angle of 40° at A.

Measure an angle of 60° at B. Extend the lines to the point where they meet.

This is an ASA construction.

# Constructions (1)

## Constructing triangles

1 Construct triangle ABC with side AB = 5 cm, side AC = 3 cm and angle CAB = 40°.

2 Construct triangle XYZ with side XZ = 7 cm, angle YXZ = 50° and angle YZX = 30°.

# 4 Constructions (2)

## Constructing lines and angles

A **perpendicular** is a line drawn at right angles to another line. A **perpendicular bisector** is a line drawn at right angles to the midpoint of another line.

**a)** Draw a line AB. Construct the **perpendicular bisector** of the line AB.

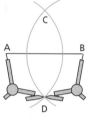

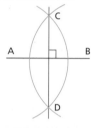

Draw long arcs of equal radius from points A and B to intersect at points C and D.

Join C and D to form the perpendicular bisector.

**b)** Draw a line AB. Construct a **perpendicular from a point** O to the line.

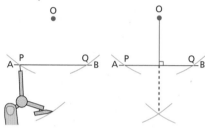

Draw two arcs from O to cross AB at P and Q, then draw an arc from P.

Draw an arc from Q using the same radius as for the arc from P and complete the perpendicular.

**c)** Construct a line **perpendicular to** PQ that passes through point A.

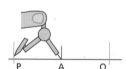

Draw a line and mark a point A. Draw two equal arcs from A to cross the line.

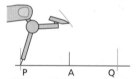

Draw an arc from P of a longer radius than the two arcs already drawn.

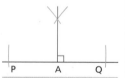

Draw an arc from Q (same radius as that drawn from P) and complete the angle.

You can construct these angles without a protractor:
- 90° by constructing a perpendicular to a point on a line
- 45° by bisecting a 90° angle
- 60° by following the steps to construct an equilateral triangle
- 30° by bisecting a 60° angle.

**Loci** are a common application of constructions.

A path is to be laid between two lamp posts, A and B, in a park. Construct the locus of points that are equidistant from the lamp posts.

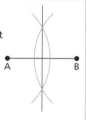

Draw the perpendicular bisector between points A and B.

**Construct the bisector of an angle.**

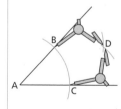

Draw an angle at point A. Draw a long arc from A to cut the lines at B and C. Draw arcs of equal radius from points B and C to intersect at point D.

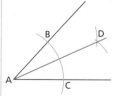

Join A to D to form the bisector of the angle.

# 4 Constructions (2)

## Constructing lines and angles

1. Construct the perpendicular bisector to line AB.

A ———————————————————— B

2. Construct an angle of 45° on the line CD.

C ———————————————————— D

# 4 Angles

## Angle facts and angles in parallel lines

Angles **on a straight line** add up to **180°**.
Angles **at a point** add up to **360°**.
**Vertically opposite** angles are **equal**.

$a + c = 180°$
$b + c = 180°$
$b + d = 180°$
$a + d = 180°$
$a + b + c + d = 360°$

$a = b$
$c = d$

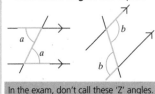

**Alternate angles** are equal.

In the exam, don't call these 'Z' angles.

**Corresponding angles** are equal.

In the exam, don't call these 'F' angles.

**Allied (co-interior) angles** sum to 180°.

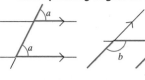

Work out the size of angle $x$.

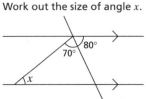

Because there are parallel lines, look out for any alternate or corresponding angles.

**Method 1**

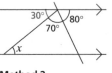

The missing angle on the straight line is 30°.

$x$ and 30° are alternate angles, so $x = 30°$

**Method 2**

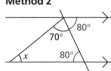

The other angle in the triangle is alternate to 80°.

Angles in a triangle add up to 180°, so $x$ is
$180° - 70° - 80° = 30°$

## Angles in polygons

Any polygon can be divided into triangles by drawing line segments from one vertex to every other vertex. To find the sum of the interior angles, multiply the number of triangles by 180°.

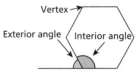

Interior angle + exterior angle = 180°

Sum of interior angles in a polygon =
(number of sides – 2) × 180°
Sum of exterior angles in a polygon = 360°

Exterior angle of a **regular** polygon =
360° ÷ (number of sides)
Interior angle of a **regular** polygon =
(sum of interior angles) ÷ (number of sides)

The diagram shows a regular hexagon ABCDEF. Work out the size of angle $x$.

Break this type of question into several steps.

Exterior angle of a regular hexagon is $\frac{360°}{6} = 60°$
Interior angle + exterior angle = 180°
Interior angle of a regular hexagon is
$180° - 60° = 120°$
So angle FED = 120°
EB bisects angle FED.
So angle BED is $\frac{120°}{2} = 60°$
Triangle EDC is isosceles.
So angle DEC is $\frac{180° - 120°}{2} = 30°$
So $x$ is 60° – 30° = 30°

# 4 Angles

## Angle facts and angles in parallel lines

1 Work out the size of the lettered angle in each diagram. Give reasons for your answers.

**a)**

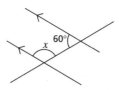

$x =$ .................... °

....................

**b)**

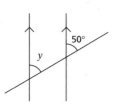

$y =$ .................... °

....................

**c)**

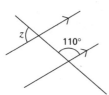

$z =$ .................... °

....................

## Angles in polygons

2 Here is an irregular polygon.

Work out the size of the largest angle.

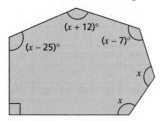

$x =$ .................... °

3 Each interior angle of a regular polygon is 176°.

Work out the number of sides in the polygon.

....................

#  Triangles and quadrilaterals

## Triangles

There are four types of triangle.

> The sum of the angles in a triangle is 180°.

| **Equilateral** triangles have three equal sides and three 60° angles. | **Isosceles** triangles have two equal sides and two equal base angles. | **Scalene** triangles have no equal sides and no equal angles. | **Right-angled** triangles have one 90° angle. |
|---|---|---|---|
|  |  |  |  |

Work out the values of angle $a$, $b$ and $c$.

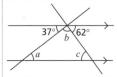

Angle $a = 37°$ ← Angle $a$ is alternate to 37°.

Angle $b = 180° - (37° + 62°) = 81°$ ← Angles on a straight line sum to 180°.

Angle $c = 180° - (37° + 81°) = 62°$ ← Angles in a triangle sum to 180°.

## Quadrilaterals

A **quadrilateral** has four sides and four angles.

> The angles in any quadrilateral add up to 360°.

| **Square** <br> • Four equal sides <br> • Four 90° angles <br> • Opposite sides are parallel <br> • Diagonals bisect each other at right angles <br>  | **Rectangle** <br> • Two pairs of equal sides <br> • Four 90° angles <br> • Opposite sides are parallel <br> • Diagonals bisect each other <br>  |
|---|---|
| **Parallelogram** <br> • Two pairs of equal sides <br> • Two pairs of equal angles <br> • Opposite sides are parallel <br> • Diagonals bisect each other <br>  | **Rhombus** <br> • Four equal sides <br> • Two pairs of equal angles <br> • Opposite sides are parallel <br> • Diagonals bisect each other at right angles <br>  |
| **Kite** <br> • Two pairs of equal sides <br> • One pair of equal angles <br> • Diagonals bisect each other at right angles <br>  | **Trapezium** <br> • One pair of parallel sides <br>  |

A rhombus is shown. Calculate the values of $x$ and $y$.

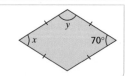

Angle $x = 70°$ ← Opposite angles in a rhombus are equal.

Angle $y$: $360° - (70° \times 2) = 220°$ ← Angles in a quadrilateral sum to 360°.

$y = 220° \div 2 = 110°$ ← Opposite angles in a rhombus are equal.

# 4 Triangles and quadrilaterals

## Triangles

1 Calculate the sizes of the lettered angles in each diagram. Give reasons for your answers.

a)

$a =$ ........................ °

........................

........................

........................

$b =$ ........................ °

........................

........................

b)

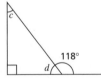

$c =$ ........................ °

........................

........................

........................

$d =$ ........................ °

........................

........................

c)

$e =$ ........................ °

........................

........................

........................

$f =$ ........................ °

........................

........................

## Quadrilaterals

2 Write down the name of a quadrilateral with one pair of equal angles. ........................

3 a) A kite is shown. Work out the values of $a$ and $b$. Give reasons for your answers.

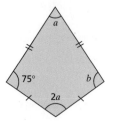

$a =$ ........................ °

........................

........................

........................

$b =$ ........................ °

........................

........................

........................

b) A trapezium is shown. Work out the sizes of angles $c$, $d$ and $e$. Give reasons for your answers.

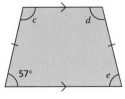

$c =$ ........................ °

........................

........................

$d =$ ........................ °

........................

........................

$e =$ ........................ °

........................

........................

#  Congruence and geometric proof

## Congruent shapes

**Congruent** shapes are the same size and the same shape. When shapes are reflected, rotated or translated, the image is congruent to the object.

**Triangles** are congruent if they satisfy any one of the following:

These shapes are congruent to each other:

| Side, Side, Side (SSS) | Side, Angle, Side (SAS) | Angle, Side, Angle (ASA) Angle, Angle, Side (AAS) | Right angle, Hypotenuse, Side (RHS) |
|---|---|---|---|
| All three sides of one triangle are equal to the three sides in the other triangle. | Two sides and the included angle of one triangle are equal to the two sides and the included angle in the other triangle. | Both triangles have two equal angles and a corresponding side that is equal in length. | Both triangles have a right angle, an equal hypotenuse and another equal side. |
| <br> | <br> | <br> | 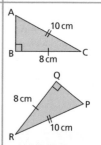 |
| AB = PQ, BC = QR, AC = PR, so congruent (SSS). | AB = PQ, AC = PR, angle A = angle P, so congruent (SAS). | Angle A = angle P, angle B = angle Q, BC = QR, so congruent (AAS). | Angle B = angle Q, AC = PR, BC = QR, so congruent (RHS). |

## Geometric proof

Geometrical proofs involve shapes and angles.

Prove that triangles ABC and PQR are congruent.

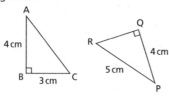

By Pythagoras' theorem, AC = 5 cm

Angle B = Angle Q = 90° (right angle)

AC = PR = 5 cm (hypotenuse)

AB = PQ = 4 cm (side)

So the triangles are congruent (RHS).

Prove that AB is equal in length to BC.

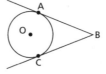

The angle between the tangents and the radius is 90° (see page 110).

Angle OAB = Angle OCB = 90°

AO = OC ← AO and OC are radii of the same circle.

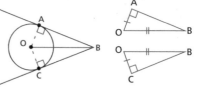

Triangles OBA and OBC are congruent by SAS.

So, AB = BC.

# Congruence and geometric proof

## Congruent shapes

1) Decide whether each pair of triangles is congruent. Give reasons for your answers.

**a)**

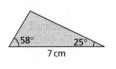

**b)**

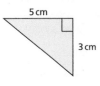

**c)**

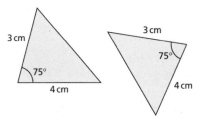

**d)**

## Geometric proof

2) Lines AC and DE are parallel. BDE is a triangle. Prove that the angles in triangle BDE sum to 180°.

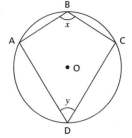

3) Prove that opposite angles in a cyclic quadrilateral add up to 180°.

# (4) Transformations

## Translation, reflection and rotation

A transformation may change a shape's position, size or orientation. The original shape is called the **object** and the transformed shape is called the **image**.

Shapes that have been translated, reflected or rotated are congruent - they are the same size but just in a different position or orientation. Points are **invariant** if they do not change after a transformation.

**Translation** of rectangle P by the vector $\begin{pmatrix} -1 \\ 3 \end{pmatrix}$.

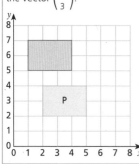

**Reflection** of rectangle Q in the line $y = x$.

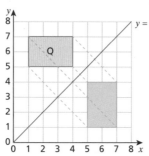

**Rotation** of triangle M 90° clockwise around the point (3, 2).

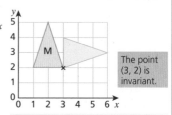

The point (3, 2) is invariant.

Trace triangle M, put your pencil on point (3, 2) and turn the tracing paper 90° clockwise. Then draw the image.

## Enlargement

Enlarging a shape makes it bigger or smaller by a given **scale factor**. Enlargement by an integer scale factor makes the shape bigger. Enlargement by a fractional scale factor makes the shape smaller. An enlarged shape is similar to the object.

An enlargement by a negative scale factor creates an upside-down image that is on the opposite side of the centre of enlargement.

An enlargement by a scale factor of -1 is the same as a rotation of 180°.

a) Enlarge triangle X by a scale factor of $\frac{1}{2}$, centre of enlargement (–3, 3). Label the image Y.

The first vertex of the object is 2 units up and 4 units to the right of the centre of enlargement. The corresponding vertex of the image is $2 \times \frac{1}{2} = 1$ unit up and $4 \times \frac{1}{2} = 2$ units to the right of the centre of enlargement. Repeat for the other vertices.

b) Enlarge triangle X by a scale factor of –2, centre of enlargement (2, 2). Label the image Z.

The distance of one vertex of the object to the centre of enlargement is $\begin{pmatrix} -3 \\ -1 \end{pmatrix}$. Multiplying each value by –2 means the distance of the corresponding vertex of the image to the centre of enlargement is $\begin{pmatrix} 6 \\ 2 \end{pmatrix}$. Repeat for the other vertices.

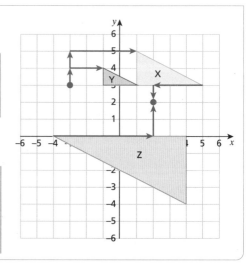

# 4 Transformations

## Translation, reflection and rotation

**1** Shape A is shown on the grid.

a) Reflect shape A in the line $x = 5$.
Label the image as shape B.

b) Rotate shape B 180° about the point (6, 1). Label the image as shape C.

c) Translate shape C by the vector $\begin{pmatrix} -2 \\ -4 \end{pmatrix}$. Label the image as shape D.

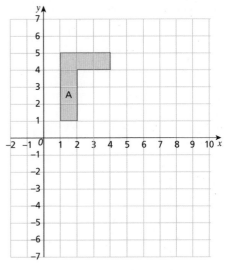

d) Describe fully the single transformation that takes shape A to shape D.

## Enlargement

**2** Enlarge shape A by a scale factor of $-\frac{1}{2}$, centre of enlargement (−1, −1).

Label the image as shape E.

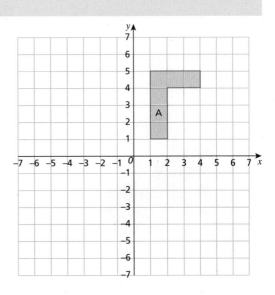

# ④ 3D shapes, plans and elevations

## 3D shapes

**3D** (or **three-dimensional**) shapes are solid figures with three dimensions – length, depth or width, and height.

For the exam you will need to work with **cubes**, **cuboids**, **prisms**, **cylinders**, **pyramids**, **cones** and **spheres**.

A prism has a constant **cross-section.** Prisms are named by the shape of their cross-section.

A pyramid has a **polygon** as its base and the faces meet at a point.

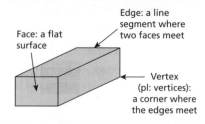

Edge: a line segment where two faces meet

Face: a flat surface

Vertex (pl: vertices): a corner where the edges meet

| Shape | | Faces | Edges | Vertices |
|---|---|---|---|---|
| Cube | Cuboid | 6 | 12 | 8 |
| Square-based pyramid | | 5 <br> 1 square and 4 triangles | 8 | 5 |
| Pentagonal prism | | 7 <br> 2 pentagons and 5 rectangles | 15 | 10 |

The number of faces, edges and vertices in a 3D shape are connected by the formula: $V - E + F = 2$, where $V$ is the number of vertices, $E$ is the number of edges and $F$ is the number of faces.

Cylinders and cones have flat surfaces and curved surfaces. A sphere has a curved surface only.

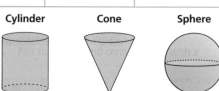

Cylinder     Cone     Sphere

## Plans and elevations

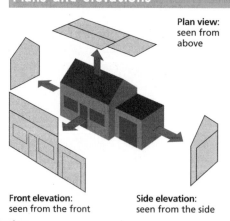

Plan view: seen from above

Front elevation: seen from the front

Side elevation: seen from the side

Draw the plan view, the front elevation and the side elevation of the 3D shape.

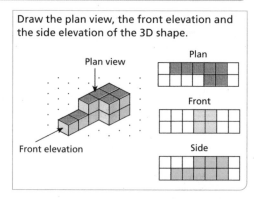

Plan view

Front elevation

Plan

Front

Side

# 4 3D shapes, plans and elevations

## 3D shapes

1. Name each shape shown below.

a)

b)
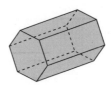

..............................................  ..............................................

c)

d)

..............................................  ..............................................

2. Complete the table to show the number of faces, edges and vertices in each shape in question 1.

|     | Shape | Faces | Edges | Vertices |
|-----|-------|-------|-------|----------|
| a)  |       |       |       |          |
| b)  |       |       |       |          |
| c)  |       |       |       |          |
| d)  |       |       |       |          |

## Plans and elevations

3. On the centimetre grid below, draw the plan view, front elevation and side elevation of the 3D shape.

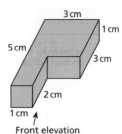

Front elevation

# 4 Scale drawings and bearings

## Scale drawings

A scale drawing is a representation of a shape or distance with accurate lengths reduced by a given **scale factor**. Scale factors can be given in words or as ratios, e.g. 1 cm represents 5 km or 1 : 500 000.

Use the map to work out the actual distance between London and Birmingham.

Scale: 1 cm represents 60 km

• Birmingham

London •

Measure the distance from London to Birmingham on the map: it is 2.8 cm.

2.8 × 60 = 168 km

The scale is 1 cm represents 60 km, so multiply the distance by 60 to find the distance in kilometres.

## Bearings

A **bearing** gives the direction to one place from another. Bearings are given using three-figures, e.g. 030° instead of 30°.

To measure a three-figure bearing:
- start from North
- measure clockwise.

If two bearings are in opposite directions, the difference between the bearings is 180°.

```
            360°
            000°
             N
315°                045°
  NW                 NE

270° W ─────╳───── E 090°

  SW                 SE
225°                135°
             S
            180°
```

The diagram shows a map drawn to scale showing two towns, A and B.

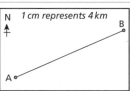

N
1 cm represents 4 km
                              B

A

a) Write the bearing from A to B.

Line the protractor up so that it is facing North and measure the angle clockwise. The angle is 67°.

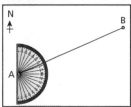

N

                  B

A

The bearing from A to B is 067°.

b) Work out the actual distance from A to B.

The real distance is 3.2 × 4 = 12.8 km

Multiply the actual distance by 4 as the scale is given as 1 cm represents 4 km.

c) Work out the bearing of A from B.

The bearing from B to A is 247°.

Given the bearing from A to B is 067°, the bearing from B to A is 180° + 067° = 247°.

# 4 Scale drawings and bearings

## Scale drawings

**1** Here is a map showing the location of some cities.

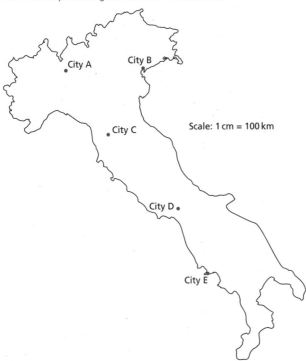

Scale: 1 cm = 100 km

Work out the distance from:

**a)** City A to City D .......................... km

**b)** City D to City E .......................... km

**c)** City B to City C .......................... km

## Bearings

**2** Using the map in question 1, write the bearing of:

**a)** City A from City D    **b)** City E from City D    **c)** City B from City C

.......................... .......................... ..........................

# 4 Perimeter and area

## Perimeter

The perimeter of a shape is the total distance around the outside edge.

A compound shape is made up from other shapes such as squares, rectangles and triangles.

When working out the perimeter of a compound shape, remember to only count the outside edges (not any edges inside the shape).

> Two shapes, A and B, are shown on a centimetre square grid. Which has the greater perimeter?

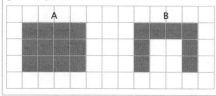

> It may help to number along the edges of the diagrams. It's not enough to just work out the perimeters. You have to state which is greater.

Perimeter of shape A is:
$4 + 3 + 4 + 3 = 14\,\text{cm}$

Perimeter of shape B is:
$3 + 1 + 2 + 2 + 2 + 1 + 3 + 4 = 18\,\text{cm}$

So shape B has the greater perimeter.

## Area

You need to know how to find the area of a triangle, trapezium and parallelogram, and how to use them to find the area of a compound shape.

> To find the area of a compound shape, break it down into its simpler component shapes and add their areas together.

**Area of triangle = $\frac{1}{2}$ × base × perpendicular height**

$A = \frac{1}{2}bh$

Perpendicular height, $h$

Base, $b$

Work out the area of each shape.

a)

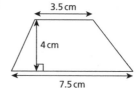

5.4 cm

6.2 cm

Area of triangle $= \frac{1}{2} \times 6.2 \times 5.4$
$= 16.74\,\text{cm}^2$

**Area of trapezium = $\frac{1}{2}(a + b)h$**

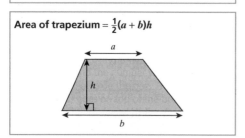

$a$

$h$

$b$

b)

3.5 cm

4 cm

7.5 cm

Area of trapezium $= \frac{1}{2} \times (3.5 + 7.5) \times 4$
$= 22\,\text{cm}^2$

**Area of a parallelogram = base × perpendicular height**

$A = bh$

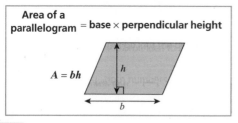

$h$

$b$

c)

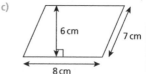

6 cm

7 cm

8 cm

> Don't mix up the perpendicular height with the sloping height.

Area of a parallelogram $= 8 \times 6$
$= 48\,\text{cm}^2$

#  Perimeter and area

## Perimeter

**1** Work out the perimeter of each shape.

**a)**

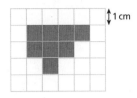

**b)**

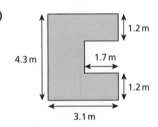

Perimeter = _____ cm          Perimeter = _____ m

## Area

**2** Work out the area of each shape.

**a)**

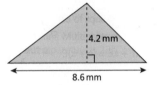

**b)**

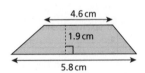

Area = _____ mm²          Area = _____ cm²

**c)**

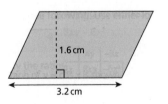

**d)**

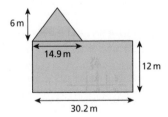

Area = _____ cm²          Area = _____ m²

# 4 Surface area and volume

## Surface area

The **surface area** of a 3D shape is the total area of all the surfaces (faces) added together. For example, the surface area of a cube is the total area of the six squares of its net.

> The surface area is equal to the area of the net of the shape. For a sphere, it is found by $4\pi r^2$

Work out the surface area of this shape.

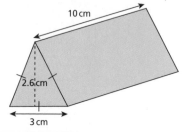

The net of a triangular prism shows that it has two triangular faces and three rectangular faces.

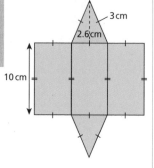

Add up the area of all the faces.

Area of each triangle is $\frac{1}{2} \times 3 \times 2.6 = 3.9\,cm^2$

Area of each rectangle is $3 \times 10 = 30\,cm^2$

Total surface area is $3.9 + 3.9 + 30 + 30 + 30 = 97.8\,cm^2$

## Volume of prisms

The **volume** of a prism is always the product of the area of the cross-section and the length (or depth) of the prism. The units for volume are cubed, e.g. $cm^3$ or $m^3$.

Cylinders are special types of prisms. The cross-section of a cylinder is a circle.

Volume of a cuboid = length × width × height

Volume of a prism = area of cross-section × length

Volume of a cylinder = $\pi \times radius^2 \times height$

Work out the volume of this triangular prism.

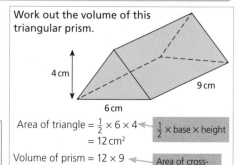

Area of triangle = $\frac{1}{2} \times 6 \times 4$  ← $\frac{1}{2} \times$ base × height

$= 12\,cm^2$

Volume of prism = $12 \times 9$  ← Area of cross-section × length

$= 108\,cm^3$

## Volume of spheres, pyramids and cones

You should also know how to use the formulae for finding the volume of spheres, pyramids and cones.

Volume of a sphere = $\frac{4}{3}\pi r^3$

Volume of a pyramid = $\frac{1}{3} \times$ area of base × vertical height

Volume of a cone = $\frac{1}{3} \times \pi r^2 h$

Work out the volume of this cone.

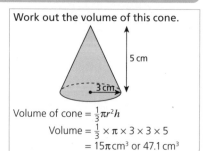

Volume of cone = $\frac{1}{3}\pi r^2 h$

Volume = $\frac{1}{3} \times \pi \times 3 \times 3 \times 5$

$= 15\pi\,cm^3$ or $47.1\,cm^3$

## Surface area

**1** Work out the surface area of each shape.

**a)**

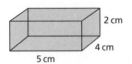

2 cm
4 cm
5 cm

Surface area = ............................ cm²

**b)**

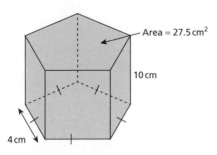

Area = 27.5 cm²

10 cm

4 cm

Surface area = ............................ cm²

## Volume of prisms

**2** Work out the volume of each shape in question 1.

**a)**

Volume = ............................ cm³

**b)**

Volume = ............................ cm³

## Volume of spheres, pyramids and cones

**3** Calculate the volume of the sphere.

6 m

Volume of a sphere = $\frac{4}{3}\pi r^3$

Volume = ............................ m³

**4** Work out the volume of the pyramid.

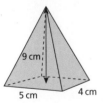

9 cm

5 cm    4 cm

Volume of a pyramid = $\frac{1}{3}$ × area of base × vertical height

Volume = ............................ cm³

# 4 Similar figures

## Similar shapes and working out lengths

Two shapes are **similar** if one shape is an enlargement of the other:
- The angles in one shape will be equal to the corresponding angles in the other shape.
- The corresponding sides of each shape are in the same ratio.

Show that triangle ACE is similar to triangle BCD.

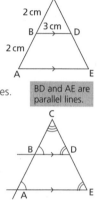

Sketching the two separate triangles will help you to visualise them.

Angle A = Angle B because they are corresponding angles.

BD and AE are parallel lines.

Similarly, angle D = angle E.

Angle C is in both triangles.

All the corresponding angles are equal, so triangle ACE is similar to triangle BCD.

Are these two triangles similar? Give reasons for your answer.

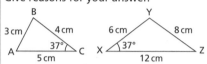

Angle X corresponds to angle C so side AB corresponds to side YZ.

Side AC corresponds to XZ and side BC corresponds to XY.

AB = 3 cm and YZ = 8 cm. $8 \div 3 = 2.\dot{6}$

XY = 6 cm and BC = 4 cm. $6 \div 4 = 1.5$

The sides are not in the same ratio, so the triangles are **not** similar.

**To work out a missing length:**
1. Work out the scale factor by dividing two corresponding lengths.
2. Multiply the known corresponding length by the scale factor.

Triangles ABC and PQR are similar. Work out the length of PR.

AB corresponds to PQ, so to find the scale factor divide PQ by AB.

$7.5 \div 5 = 1.5$

AC corresponds to PR, so the length of PR is $8 \times 1.5 = 12$ cm

## Area and volume of similar figures

For similar shapes with lengths in the ratio $1 : n$, the ratio of the areas is $1 : n^2$.

For similar solids with lengths in the ratio $1 : n$, the ratio of the volumes is $1 : n^3$.

These rectangles are similar with a scale factor of 2. Work out the area of the larger rectangle.

Area of the smaller rectangle
$= 4\,\text{cm} \times 6\,\text{cm} = 24\,\text{cm}^2$

Area of the larger rectangle
$= 24 \times 2^2 = 96\,\text{cm}^2$

Multiply by the scale factor squared.

These cuboids are similar, scale factor $\frac{1}{4}$. Work out the volume of the smaller cuboid.

 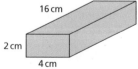

Volume of the larger cuboid =
$2\,\text{cm} \times 4\,\text{cm} \times 16\,\text{cm} = 128\,\text{cm}^3$

Volume of the smaller cuboid $= 128 \times \left(\frac{1}{4}\right)^3$
$= 128 \div 64 = 2\,\text{cm}^3$

##  Similar figures

## Similar shapes and working out lengths

**1** Show that these two triangles are similar.

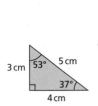
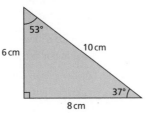

..............................................................................................................

..............................................................................................................

..............................................................................................................

..............................................................................................................

**2** Work out the length of CE in the diagram below.

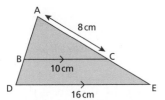

CE = ................................ cm

## Area and volume of similar figures

**3** Here are two similar rectangles, A and B.

**B**

**A**

Area = 400 m²

Area = 25 m²

Work out the linear scale factor of enlargement from rectangle A to B. ................................

**4** These prisms are similar.

Work out the volume of the larger prism.

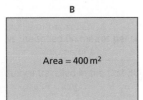

4 cm

12 cm

Volume = 30 cm³

Volume = ........................ cm³

# 4 Circles

## Circle facts

- The **circumference** of a circle is the distance around the edge of the circle (its perimeter).
- The **radius** of a circle is a straight line from the centre to the circumference.
- The **diameter** is a straight line through the centre joining opposite points on the circumference.
- A **chord** is a straight line joining any two points on the circumference.

- A **tangent** is a straight line that touches the circumference of a circle.
- An **arc** is a part of the circumference of a circle.
- A **sector** is the area enclosed by two radii and an arc.
- A **segment** is the area between a chord and its arc.

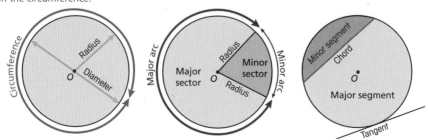

## Circumference and area of circles

Circumference = $\pi \times$ diameter or $C = \pi d$

Circumference = $2 \times \pi \times$ radius or $C = 2\pi r$

Area = $\pi \times$ radius²

$A = \pi r^2$

a) Calculate the circumference of this circle to 2 decimal places.

$C = 2\pi r$

$= 2 \times \pi \times 5.4$

$= 33.929...$

$= 33.93$ cm

5.4 cm

$O$

You could get the same answer by working out the diameter ($2 \times 5.4 = 10.8$ cm), then using the formula $C = \pi d$.

b) Work out the area of the circle to 2 decimal places.

$A = \pi r^2 = \pi \times 5.4 \times 5.4$

$= 91.608...$

$= 91.61$ cm²

## Sector area and arc length

A **sector** is a fraction of a circle, so the sector area is a fraction of the area.

Area of sector = $\frac{\text{angle at centre}}{360°} \times$ area of circle

An **arc** is a fraction of the perimeter of the circle, so the arc length is a fraction of the circumference.

Arc length = $\frac{\text{angle at centre}}{360°} \times$ circumference of circle

Work out the arc length and the area of the sector to 1 decimal place.

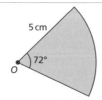

5 cm

72°

$O$

Arc length = $\frac{\text{angle at centre}}{360°} \times$ circumference of circle

$= \frac{72°}{360°} \times 2 \times \pi \times 5 = 6.3$ cm

Area of sector = $\frac{\text{angle at centre}}{360°} \times$ area of circle

$= \frac{72°}{360°} \times \pi \times 5^2 = 15.7$ cm²

## Circle facts

1 Label the parts of the circle shown.

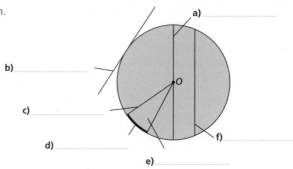

a) ............................

b) ............................

c) ............................

d) ............................

e) ............................

f) ............................

## Circumference and area of circles

2 Work out the circumference and area of each circle, giving your answers to 1 decimal place.

a)

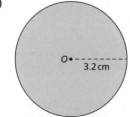

$O\bullet\text{-------}$ 3.2 cm

Circumference = ............................ cm

Area = ............................ cm²

b)

$O$
5.8 m

Circumference = ............................ m

Area = ............................ m²

## Sector area and arc length

3 A sector is shown.

Work out the following, giving your answers to 2 decimal places.

120°

O   5 cm

a) The arc length of the sector

............................ cm

b) The area of the sector

............................ cm²

# 4 Circle theorems

## Tangents and chords

A **tangent** is a straight line that touches the circle at a single point on the circumference.
A **chord** is a straight line drawn from one part of the circumference to another.

The angle between a tangent and the radius at the point on the circumference is 90°.

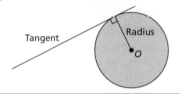

A radius drawn **perpendicular** (at 90°) to a chord bisects the chord.

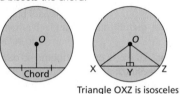

Triangle OXZ is isosceles

Tangents to a circle drawn from the same point are equal in length. The triangles formed using tangents from a common point, radii and a line drawn from the centre are **congruent** right-angled triangles.

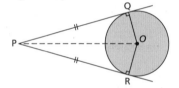

To understand circle theorems, you need to understand the word **subtended**.

This diagram shows an angle $x$ **subtended** by an arc.

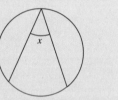

## Angles

The angle at the centre of a circle is twice the angle at the circumference that is subtended by the same arc.

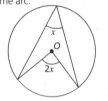

Any angle at the circumference that is subtended by a diameter is 90°.

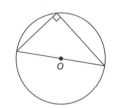

Angles at the circumference, in the same segment and subtended by the same arc, are equal.

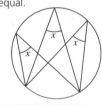

A **cyclic quadrilateral** is a quadrilateral with all four vertices on the circumference of a circle.

Opposite angles of a cyclic quadrilateral add up to 180°.

$x + y = 180°$

$a + b = 180°$

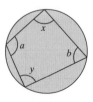

The **alternate segment theorem** states that the angle between a tangent and a chord through the point of contact is equal to the angle at the circumference in the **alternate segment**, subtended by the chord.

# 4 Circle theorems

## Tangents and chords

1 Prove that triangle OYX is congruent to triangle OZX.

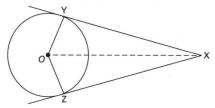

......................................................................................

......................................................................................

......................................................................................

......................................................................................

......................................................................................

## Angles

2 Work out the size of the lettered angle in each part, giving reasons with your answers.

**a)**

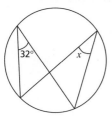

$x =$ .................... °

......................................................................................

......................................................................................

**b)**

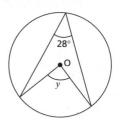

$y =$ .................... °

......................................................................................

......................................................................................

**c)**

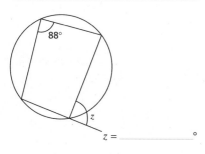

$z =$ .................... °

......................................................................................

......................................................................................

**d)**

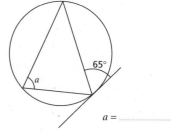

$a =$ .................... °

......................................................................................

......................................................................................

# 4 Pythagoras' theorem

## Pythagoras in right-angled triangles

In a **right-angled triangle**, the side opposite the right angle is called the **hypotenuse**.

Pythagoras' theorem states that the square on the hypotenuse is equal to the sum of the squares on the other two sides.

> Pythagoras theorem is $a^2 + b^2 = c^2$ where $c$ is the hypotenuse and $a$ and $b$ are the other two sides.

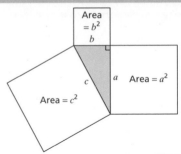

Area $= b^2$

$b$

$c$ $a$ Area $= a^2$

Area $= c^2$

Work out the length of the hypotenuse in this triangle.

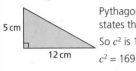

5 cm

12 cm

Pythagoras' theorem states that $c^2 = a^2 + b^2$

So $c^2$ is $12^2 + 5^2 = 144 + 25$

$c^2 = 169$

So $c$ is $\sqrt{169} = 13$ cm

Calculate the missing side length in this triangle.

29 m

21 m

$a^2 + b^2 = c^2$

$21^2 + b^2 = 29^2$

$b^2 = 29^2 - 21^2$

$b = \sqrt{29^2 - 21^2} = 20$ m

## Using Pythagoras' theorem to solve problems, including in 3D

Work out the area of this isosceles triangle.

An isosceles triangle can be split into two right-angled triangles, so you can use Pythagoras' theorem to work out the height. You then have all the information to work out the area.

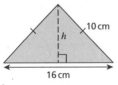

10 cm

$h$

16 cm

So $10^2 = h^2 + 8^2$

$100 = h^2 + 64$

$100 - 64 = h^2$

$36 = h^2$

So $h = 6$ cm

Area $= \frac{1}{2} \times 16 \times 6 = 48$ cm²

$h$ 10 cm

8 cm

$\frac{1}{2} \times$ base $\times$ height

To use Pythagoras' theorem in 3D, break down the shape into right-angled triangles that you can more easily work with in 2D.

> To find the diagonal of a cuboid, you can also use the formula $a^2 + b^2 + c^2 = d^2$ where $d$ is the diagonal and $a$, $b$ and $c$ are the side lengths of the cuboid.

Work out the length of the diagonal in this cuboid.

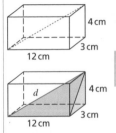

4 cm

3 cm

12 cm

$d$

4 cm

3 cm

12 cm

There are several right-angled triangles in this cuboid.

$c$ 4 cm

3 cm

$d$

$c$

12 cm

Draw the right-angled triangles on their own

By Pythagoras' theorem, $c = 5$ cm.

Use the length found for side $c$ to find side $d$.

$d^2 = 12^2 + 5^2 = 144 + 25 = 169$

$d = \sqrt{169} = 13$, therefore the diagonal is 13 cm.

# 4 Pythagoras' theorem

## Pythagoras in right-angled triangles

1 Work out the lettered side length in each triangle.

**a)** Give your answer to 2 decimal places.

$x =$ _____

**b)**

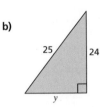

$y =$ _____

## Using Pythagoras' theorem to solve problems, including in 3D

2 This compound shape is made up of four triangles and a square.

Work out the area of the shape.

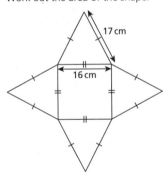

_____ cm²

3 Work out the length of the diagonal of this cuboid.

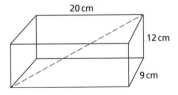

_____ cm

# (4) Trigonometry

## Working out sides and angles

**Trigonometry** is used to work out unknown lengths or unknown angles in **right-angled triangles**:

- The **hypotenuse** is opposite the right angle.
- The **opposite side** is opposite the marked angle ($x$).
- The **adjacent side** is next to the marked angle ($x$).

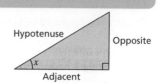

The three trigonometrical ratios you need to know are called **sine**, **cosine** and **tangent**.

Remember SOH CAH TOA.     $\sin x = \dfrac{\text{opposite}}{\text{hypotenuse}}$     $\cos x = \dfrac{\text{adjacent}}{\text{hypotenuse}}$     $\tan x = \dfrac{\text{opposite}}{\text{adjacent}}$

You need to know the exact values of $\sin \theta$ and $\cos \theta$ for $\theta = 0°, 30°, 45°, 60°$ and $90°$.
And you need to know the exact values of $\tan \theta$ for $\theta = 0°, 30°, 45°$ and $60°$.

**To work out a length using trigonometry:**
1. Label the sides (hyp, opp, adj) in this order.
2. Circle the given side and the one to be found.
3. Choose the correct ratio.
4. Set up and solve the equation.

**To work out an angle using trigonometry:**
1. Label the sides (hyp, opp, adj) in this order.
2. Circle the two given sides.
3. Choose the correct ratio.
4. Set up and solve the equation.

To find a missing angle, ensure you can work with inverse trigonometric ratios on your calculator.

Work out the length $x$.

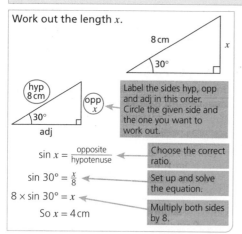

Label the sides hyp, opp and adj in this order. Circle the given side and the one you want to work out.

$\sin x = \dfrac{\text{opposite}}{\text{hypotenuse}}$ ← Choose the correct ratio.

$\sin 30° = \dfrac{x}{8}$ ← Set up and solve the equation.

$8 \times \sin 30° = x$ ←

So $x = 4$ cm ← Multiply both sides by 8.

Work out the size of angle $x$.

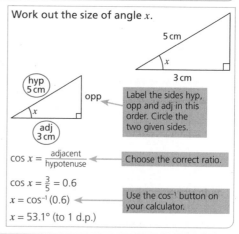

Label the sides hyp, opp and adj in this order. Circle the two given sides.

$\cos x = \dfrac{\text{adjacent}}{\text{hypotenuse}}$ ← Choose the correct ratio.

$\cos x = \dfrac{3}{5} = 0.6$

$x = \cos^{-1}(0.6)$ ← Use the cos⁻¹ button on your calculator.

$x = 53.1°$ (to 1 d.p.)

## Trigonometry in 3D

The diagram shows a square-based pyramid. The sides of the square base are 6 cm. The sloping edges are 5 cm.

Work out the angle VMX (marked $\theta$).

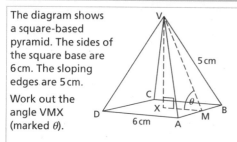

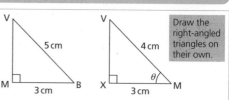

Draw the right-angled triangles on their own.

Looking at triangle VBM, by Pythagoras VM is 4 cm.

Looking at triangle VMX gives $\cos \theta = \dfrac{3}{4}$

So $\theta = 41.4°$ (to 1 d.p.)

**Trigonometry**

## Working out sides and angles

1 Work out the value of $x$ in each diagram. Give your answers to 2 decimal places where appropriate.

**a)**

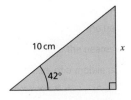

............................ cm

**b)**

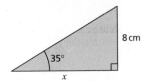

............................ cm

**c)**

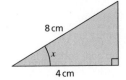

............................ °

## Trigonometry in 3D

2 Here is a cuboid, ABCDEFGH.

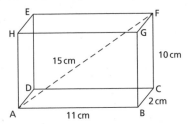

The length of the diagonal AF = 15 cm.

Work out the angle between AF and the plane ABCD.
Give your answer to 2 significant figures.

............................ °

# 4 Sine, cosine and area rules

## Sine rule and cosine rule

The sine rule and cosine rule can be used to work out unknown lengths and angles in triangles that are **not** right-angled.

In a triangle that is not right-angled, the angles can be labelled $A$, $B$ and $C$. The sides opposite each angle can be labelled $a$, $b$ and $c$.

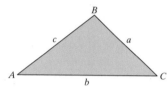

The **sine rule** can be used when you know both values for a particular letter (e.g. $A$ and $a$) and one other value.

The **cosine rule** can be used when you know two sides and an angle between them, or all three sides.

The sine rule is:
$$\frac{a}{\sin A} = \frac{b}{\sin B} = \frac{c}{\sin C} \quad \text{or} \quad \frac{\sin A}{a} = \frac{\sin B}{b} = \frac{\sin C}{c}$$
The cosine rule for finding a missing side is
$$a^2 = b^2 + c^2 - 2bc \cos A$$
This can be rearranged to find a missing angle:
$$\cos A = \frac{b^2 + c^2 - a^2}{2bc}$$

**To use the sine and cosine rules:**
1. Label the sides and angles.
2. Write out the formula.
3. Circle the parts you know.
4. Set up and solve the equation.

## Area rule

To find the area of any triangle when you know two sides and the angle between them, use the rule:

Area of triangle $= \frac{1}{2}ab \sin C$

**Calculate the area of the triangle. Give your answer to 2 significant figures.**

$$\text{Area} = \frac{1}{2}ab \sin C$$
$$= \frac{1}{2} \times 3 \times 8 \times \sin 45°$$
$$= 8.5 \text{ cm}^2 \text{ (to 2 s.f.)}$$

---

**a)** Work out the length of $AC$.

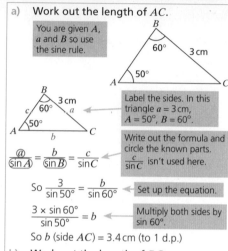

You are given $A$, $a$ and $B$ so use the sine rule.

Label the sides. In this triangle $a = 3$ cm, $A = 50°$, $B = 60°$.

Write out the formula and circle the known parts. $\frac{c}{\sin C}$ isn't used here.

$$\frac{a}{\sin A} = \frac{b}{\sin B} = \frac{c}{\sin C}$$

So $\dfrac{3}{\sin 50°} = \dfrac{b}{\sin 60°}$ ← Set up the equation.

$\dfrac{3 \times \sin 60°}{\sin 50°} = b$ ← Multiply both sides by $\sin 60°$.

So $b$ (side $AC$) $= 3.4$ cm (to 1 d.p.)

**b)** Work out the length of $BC$.

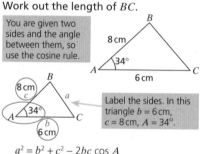

You are given two sides and the angle between them, so use the cosine rule.

Label the sides. In this triangle $b = 6$ cm, $c = 8$ cm, $A = 34°$.

$$a^2 = b^2 + c^2 - 2bc \cos A$$
So $a^2 = 6^2 + 8^2 - (2 \times 6 \times 8 \cos 34°)$
$a^2 = 20.4...$ ← $a =$ the square root of $20.4...$
So $a$ (side $BC$) $= 4.52$ cm (to 1 d.p.)

**c)** Work out the size of angle $A$.

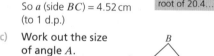

You are given all three sides so use the cosine rule.

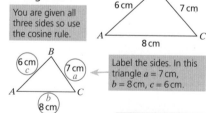

Label the sides. In this triangle $a = 7$ cm, $b = 8$ cm, $c = 6$ cm.

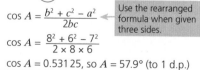

$$\cos A = \frac{b^2 + c^2 - a^2}{2bc}$$

Use the rearranged formula when given three sides.

$$\cos A = \frac{8^2 + 6^2 - 7^2}{2 \times 8 \times 6}$$

$\cos A = 0.53125$, so $A = 57.9°$ (to 1 d.p.)

# 4 Sine, cosine and area rules

## Sine rule and cosine rule

**1** Calculate the lettered sides and angles. Give your answers to 1 decimal place.

**a)**

$x =$ .................................. cm

**b)**

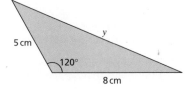

$y =$ .................................. cm

**c)**

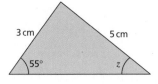

$z =$ .................................. °

## Area rule

**2** Calculate the area of this triangle.

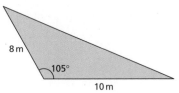

Area = .................................. m²

# 4 Vectors

## Introduction to vectors

A **vector** is line segment of a certain length (magnitude) and a particular direction.

A **scalar** is a number with magnitude only and no direction.

A vector can be written using an arrow to show its direction between two points, e.g. $\overrightarrow{AB}$, or it can be written with a bold, lowercase letter, e.g. **a**. When writing a vector by hand, underline the letter, e.g. $\underline{a}$.

A vector can be represented in **column notation**, which tells you the magnitude in each direction, $\begin{pmatrix} \text{change in } x \\ \text{change in } y \end{pmatrix}$.

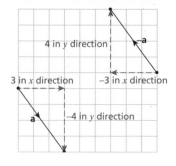

Vectors are equal if they have the same length and direction, no matter where they are on a grid.
A negative vector has the same magnitude as another vector but the opposite direction.

## Calculating with vectors

**Adding and subtracting vectors:**
1. Draw the vectors 'nose to tail' so that they join up.
2. Add them to find the resultant vector.
3. To subtract a vector on a diagram, reverse the direction.

When adding vectors, $\overrightarrow{AB} + \overrightarrow{BC} = \overrightarrow{AC}$

A vector that has been **multiplied by a scalar** (a number) is a multiple of that vector in the same direction. Here the vector $\overrightarrow{CD} = 2 \times \overrightarrow{AB}$.

$\mathbf{a} = \begin{pmatrix} 4 \\ 3 \end{pmatrix}$ and $\mathbf{b} = \begin{pmatrix} 3 \\ -1 \end{pmatrix}$

a) Write **a** + **b** as a column vector.

$\mathbf{a} + \mathbf{b} = \begin{pmatrix} 4 \\ 3 \end{pmatrix} + \begin{pmatrix} 3 \\ -1 \end{pmatrix}$

$= \begin{pmatrix} 4+3 \\ 3-1 \end{pmatrix} = \begin{pmatrix} 7 \\ 2 \end{pmatrix}$

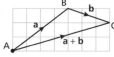

b) Write **a** − **b** as a column vector.

$\mathbf{a} - \mathbf{b} = \begin{pmatrix} 4 \\ 3 \end{pmatrix} - \begin{pmatrix} 3 \\ -1 \end{pmatrix}$

$= \begin{pmatrix} 4-3 \\ 3+1 \end{pmatrix} = \begin{pmatrix} 1 \\ 4 \end{pmatrix}$

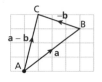

In triangle OAB, $\overrightarrow{OA} = \mathbf{a}$, $\overrightarrow{OB} = \mathbf{b}$. The point X divides the line AB in the ratio 2 : 1.

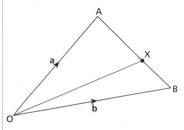

a) Work out vector $\overrightarrow{AB}$ in terms of **a** and **b**.

$\overrightarrow{AB} = \overrightarrow{AO} + \overrightarrow{OB} = -\mathbf{a} + \mathbf{b}$

b) Work out vector $\overrightarrow{OX}$ in terms of **a** and **b**.

$\overrightarrow{AX} = \tfrac{2}{3} \overrightarrow{AB}$

$\overrightarrow{AX} = -\tfrac{2}{3}\mathbf{a} + \tfrac{2}{3}\mathbf{b}$

$\overrightarrow{OX} = \overrightarrow{OA} + \overrightarrow{AX}$

$\overrightarrow{OX} = \mathbf{a} - \tfrac{2}{3}\mathbf{a} + \tfrac{2}{3}\mathbf{b}$

$\overrightarrow{OX} = \tfrac{1}{3}\mathbf{a} + \tfrac{2}{3}\mathbf{b}$

## Introduction to vectors

**1** A is the point (1, 2).

Vector $\overrightarrow{AB} = \begin{pmatrix} 5 \\ -3 \end{pmatrix}$

Work out the coordinates of B.

## Calculating with vectors

**2** ABCDEF is a regular hexagon made up of six equilateral triangles.

$\overrightarrow{AB} = \mathbf{a}$ and $\overrightarrow{BC} = \mathbf{b}$

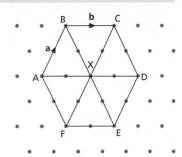

Express the following vectors in terms of **a** and **b**.

**a)** $\overrightarrow{ED}$

**b)** $\overrightarrow{FC}$

**c)** $\overrightarrow{FD}$

**d)** $\overrightarrow{XB}$

**3** $\overrightarrow{OA} = \mathbf{a}$    $\overrightarrow{OB} = \mathbf{b}$    $\overrightarrow{OC} = 2\mathbf{a} - 3\mathbf{b}$

Work out the following vectors.

**a)** $\overrightarrow{BA}$

**b)** $\overrightarrow{AC}$

**c)** $\overrightarrow{CB}$

# ⑤ Theoretical probability

## Probability of single events

**Probability** is the chance or likelihood of something happening on a scale from 0 to 1.

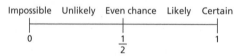

Impossible   Unlikely   Even chance   Likely   Certain

0 ········· $\frac{1}{2}$ ········· 1

> Probabilities can be written as fractions, decimals or percentages.

An **event** is anything used to measure the probability of something, e.g. rolling a dice.

An **outcome** is the result of an event, e.g. rolling a 2.

The **sample space** is the set of all possible outcomes of an event, e.g. rolling a 1, 2, 3, 4, 5, or 6 on a six-sided dice. Sample spaces are often shown using tables or lists.

**Equally likely outcomes** have the same probability of happening, e.g. rolling a 3 or rolling a 4 on a fair, six-sided dice both have a probability of $\frac{1}{6}$.

**Theoretical probability** is when probability is calculated based on the number of ways an outcome can occur. This contrasts with experimental probability (see page 122).

The theoretical probability of an outcome can be found using the formula:

$$P(\text{outcome}) = \frac{\text{number of ways the outcome can happen}}{\text{total number of possible outcomes}}$$

**Mutually exclusive events** cannot happen at the same time. For example, if you choose an odd or an even number from a list of integers, you can only choose one or the other (not both).

> If events are mutually exclusive, the probability of an outcome $p$ **not** happening is $1 - p$.

Work out the probability of obtaining a sum of 10 when rolling two dice.

|  |  | Dice 1 |  |  |  |  |  |
|---|---|---|---|---|---|---|---|
|  |  | **1** | **2** | **3** | **4** | **5** | **6** |
| **Dice 2** | **1** | 2 | 3 | 4 | 5 | 6 | 7 |
|  | **2** | 3 | 4 | 5 | 6 | 7 | 8 |
|  | **3** | 4 | 5 | 6 | 7 | 8 | 9 |
|  | **4** | 5 | 6 | 7 | 8 | 9 | ⑩ |
|  | **5** | 6 | 7 | 8 | 9 | ⑩ | 11 |
|  | **6** | 7 | 8 | 9 | ⑩ | 11 | 12 |

To find all the possible outcomes, make a table showing the outcome of the first dice, the second dice and their sum.

There are three ways to roll a sum of 10.

$P(\text{sum of 10}) = \frac{3}{36}$ or $\frac{1}{12}$

There are $6 \times 6 = 36$ possible outcomes.

## Probability of combined events

**Combined events** are when more than one event occur to give an outcome, e.g. rolling a dice and flipping a coin.

Two events are **independent** if the outcome of one event does not affect the outcome of the

other event, e.g. rolling a dice does not affect the outcome of flipping a coin.

> If two events are independent,
> $P(A \text{ and } B) = P(A) \times P(B)$

A coin is flipped and a fair, six-sided dice numbered 1 to 6 is rolled. Work out the probability of getting tails and an odd number.

|  |  | Dice |  |  |  |  |  |
|---|---|---|---|---|---|---|---|
|  |  | **1** | **2** | **3** | **4** | **5** | **6** |
| **Coin** | **Heads** | H, 1 | H, 2 | H, 3 | H, 4 | H, 5 | H, 6 |
|  | **Tails** | ⓉⓁ | T, 2 | Ⓣ③ | T, 4 | Ⓣ⑤ | T, 6 |

There are three outcomes for tails and an odd number.

$P(\text{tails and odd}) = \frac{3}{12} = \frac{1}{4}$

There are 12 total outcomes.

Using the product rule for independent events, $P(\text{tails and odd}) = P(\text{tails}) \times P(\text{odd}) = \frac{1}{2} \times \frac{1}{2} = \frac{1}{4}$

# 5 Theoretical probability

## Probability of single events

**1** A game is played by rolling two fair, six-sided dice and finding their product.

**a)** Draw a sample space diagram to show the possible outcomes.

**b)** Work out the probability that the product is 4. ......................................

**c)** Work out the probability that the product is **not** 12. ......................................

## Probability of combined events

**2** Two spinners are spun. The first spinner is numbered 1 to 4. The second spinner has four sections: two red, one blue and one yellow.

**a)** Draw a sample space diagram showing the possible outcomes.

**b)** Calculate the probability of getting a 4 and landing on red.

......................................

# 5 Experimental probability

## Probability experiments

**Experimental probability** is useful when it is not possible to find a theoretical probability (see page 120), such as when predicting the weather. Trials are performed and results are recorded to find an **estimated probability** or **relative frequency**.

Experimental probability can also be used to determine **fairness** or **bias**.

A trial or experiment is fair or unbiased when each outcome is equally likely. It is biased when the outcomes are not equally likely.

The relative frequency of an event is an estimated probability, based on the outcomes of an experiment. The sum of the relative frequencies of all possible outcomes is 1.

Relative frequency = $\frac{\text{number of times outcome occurred}}{\text{total number of trials}}$

> The experimental probability will get closer to the theoretical probability the more an unbiased experiment is performed or the more a sample size is increased.

Jo suspects a dice is biased towards landing on 3.

a) Write the theoretical probability of the dice landing on 3.

$P(3) = \frac{1}{6}$ or $0.1\dot{6}$

b) Jo rolls the dice 100 times and records the results in the table below. Write the relative frequency of the dice landing on 3.

| Number | 1 | 2 | 3 | 4 | 5 | 6 |
|---|---|---|---|---|---|---|
| Frequency | 14 | 15 | 22 | 18 | 15 | 16 |

Relative frequency = $\frac{22}{100}$ or 0.22

c) Jo rolls the dice another 100 times and it lands on 3 on 12 occasions. Calculate the new relative frequency.

Relative frequency = $\frac{34}{200}$ or 0.17

> $\frac{34}{200}$ is a better estimate of the probability of rolling a 3 than $\frac{22}{100}$ because it is based on more trials.

d) Is Jo correct to think the dice is biased?

The dice does not appear to be biased as the relative frequency after 200 trials is close to the theoretical probability.

## Expected outcomes

**Expected frequency** involves calculating the number of times you expect an outcome to occur.

Expected frequency = number of trials × probability of the event

Estimate the number of times you would expect the spinner to land on red if it were spun:

a) 5 times

$P(red) = \frac{2}{8} = \frac{1}{4}$

Expected frequency = $5 \times \frac{1}{4} = 1.25$

> The expected frequency does not have to be an integer.

b) 20 times

Expected frequency = $20 \times \frac{1}{4} = 5$

c) Mo spins the spinner 20 times and gets red 8 times. He decides the spinner is biased. Do you agree?

Although 8 is greater than 5, he should spin the spinner more times to decide if it is biased. 20 is not a very large sample size.

This spinner is used in a fairground game. It costs £1 to play. Players win £4 if the spinner lands on blue and £2 if it lands on green. How much money should Bilal expect to win if he plays 10 times?

$P(\text{winning } £4) = \frac{1}{8}$

> There is one blue section out of eight.

$P(\text{winning } £2) = \frac{2}{8} = \frac{1}{4}$

Expected number of £4 wins = $10 \times \frac{1}{8} = 1.25$

> He plays 10 times and the probability of winning £4 is $\frac{1}{8}$

Expected number of £2 wins = $10 \times \frac{1}{4} = 2.5$

Expected winnings
= $(1.25 \times £4) + (2.5 \times £2)$
= £10

> He can expect to win £4 on 1.25 occasions and £2 on 2.5 occasions. Paying £10 to play the game, he can expect to win his money back.

# Experimental probability

## Probability experiments

**1** Belle spins a spinner and records the results in a table.

| Colour | Blue | Red | Green | Yellow |
|---|---|---|---|---|
| Frequency | 15 | 20 | | |
| Relative frequency | 0.25 | | 0.30 | |

Complete the table. Give the relative frequencies to 2 decimal places.

## Expected outcomes

**2** Students in Amira's class count butterflies in their gardens over a period of one week. The table shows the results.

| Species | Red admiral | Gatekeeper | Large white | Small white | Meadow brown |
|---|---|---|---|---|---|
| Frequency | 26 | 19 | 22 | 18 | 15 |

**a)** Calculate the relative frequency of red admiral butterflies.

**b)** If there are 700 butterflies in Amira's local park, estimate how many of them will be red admirals.

**3** A game is played with a fair, six-sided dice numbered 1 to 6.

If a player rolls a 3 or a 6, they move forward one space.
If they roll a 2, they move back one space.
If they roll another number, they do not move at all.

How many spaces forward can a player expect to move in 20 turns?

# 5 Tree diagrams

## Frequency trees

A **frequency tree** shows the frequency of the outcomes (or sample space) of two events. Branches show the outcomes of each event.

> The probability of each outcome is the experimental probability, or relative frequency.

**To draw a frequency tree:**

1. Start with a single point. Draw branches for each possible outcome.
2. Write the outcomes at the end of each branch.
3. Write the frequency on each branch.
4. Repeat for each event, starting with the outcome of the previous event.

In a school, there are 10 maths teachers and 12 science teachers.
7 of the maths teachers like tea. 5 of the science teachers do not like tea.

a) Draw a frequency tree to represent the sample space.

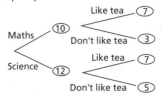

b) How many maths and science teachers do not like tea in total?

3 maths teachers and 5 science teachers don't like tea, so 8 teachers do not like tea.

c) Calculate the probability that a person chosen at random from the maths and science teachers does not like tea.

8 teachers out of 22 do not like tea, so P(teacher does not like tea) = $\frac{8}{22}$ or $\frac{4}{11}$

## Tree diagrams

A tree diagram is similar to a frequency tree; however, it shows the probability of each event rather than the frequency. It is especially useful for calculating probabilities of dependent events.

> To work out the probability of combined events, multiply the probability of the outcomes along each branch.

**To draw a tree diagram:**

1. Start with a single point. Draw branches corresponding to the possible outcomes.
2. Write the outcomes of the first event at the end of each branch.
3. Work out the probability of each outcome and write it on each branch. The probabilities of each set of branches should sum to 1.
4. Repeat for each event, starting with the outcome of the previous event.

At a school, students have either a school dinner or bring packed lunch. The probability of a student ordering a school dinner is 0.3. Two students are chosen at random.

a) Use a tree diagram to work out the probability of both students ordering school dinners.

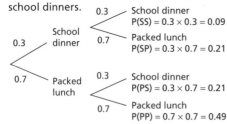

P(SS) = P(1st school dinner) × P(2nd school dinner) = 0.3 × 0.3 = 0.09   P(A and B) = P(A) × P(B)

b) Use the tree diagram to work out the probability of exactly one of the students ordering school dinners.

> There are two ways this outcome can occur. The first student could order school dinner and the second student have packed lunch, or vice-versa.

P(exactly one school dinner) = P(PS) + P(SP)

= 0.21 + 0.21

= 0.42

# ⑤ Tree diagrams

## Frequency trees

**1** A yoga and Pilates studio has 180 members.

80 members attend classes in the morning and the remaining members attend classes in the evening.
Of the members who attend in the morning, 30 prefer yoga and the rest prefer Pilates.
Of the evening members, 40 prefer Pilates and the rest prefer yoga.

**a)** Draw a frequency tree to show this information.

**b)** Calculate the probability that a member chosen at random prefers Pilates classes.

......................................

## Tree diagrams

**2** A factory produces mechanical parts. The probability that a part is **not** defective is 0.98

Two parts are chosen at random. Use a tree diagram to work out the probability of:

**a)** both parts being defective

......................................

**b)** at least one part **not** being defective.

......................................

## Interpreting Venn diagrams

A **set** is a collection of things (elements), e.g. all the even numbers up to 20 or the factors of 30.

A **Venn diagram** shows the relationship between two or more sets and is a visual representation of what they have and do not have in common. The **universal set**, ξ, is the set containing all elements.

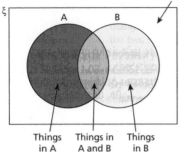

Things not in A or B

ξ

Things in A    Things in A and B    Things in B

The **intersection**, $A \cap B$, holds the elements that are in both set A and in set B.

The **union**, $A \cup B$, holds the elements that are in at least one of set A and set B.

The **complement** of a set, A', holds the elements that are **not** in set A.

This Venn diagram shows which shifts some members of staff work at a company.

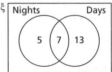

ξ  Nights    Days

5  7  13

a) How many members of staff work night shifts?

Add the numbers in the 'Nights' circle: the 5 who work nights only and the 7 in the intersection who work both nights and days.

5 + 7 = 12 staff work night shifts

b) How many members of staff does the company have in total?

The company has a total of 5 + 7 + 13 = 25 staff

Add up all the numbers in the Venn diagram.

c) What is the probability that a member of staff chosen at random works both night and day shifts?

P(both shifts) = $\frac{7}{25}$

7 out of 25 workers work both shifts.

If using a Venn diagram to calculate probabilities:

$$P(A) = \frac{\text{number of things in set A}}{\text{total number of things in the universal set}}$$

## Drawing Venn diagrams

**To draw a Venn diagram:**

1. Draw overlapping circles representing each set and label them.
2. Fill in any sections that can be completed without calculation from the information given.
3. Work out the outstanding sections (e.g. a value in the intersection may enable you to find a missing value for one of the circles).
4. Check your final diagram against any totals given in the question.

There are 28 students in a class:

- 12 students study Spanish.
- 15 students study French.
- 3 students study both French and Spanish.
- The rest do not study either language.

a) Draw a Venn diagram to show this information.

b) Use the Venn diagram to work out the probability that a randomly chosen student studies only French.

P(only French) = $\frac{12}{28}$ or $\frac{3}{7}$

3 students study both French and Spanish.

ξ

S    F

9  3  12

4

Of the 15 students that study French, 3 study both French and Spanish, so there are 15 − 3 = 12 students who study only French.

12 + 15 − 3 = 24 students who study French and/or Spanish, so there are 4 who do not study either language.

# 5 ) Venn diagrams

## Interpreting Venn diagrams

**1** Some students were asked whether they play football (F), rugby (R), or both.
The Venn diagram shows the results.

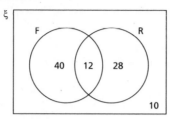

**a)** How many students were surveyed?

**b)** How many students said they only play football?

**c)** What is the probability that a student chosen at random plays rugby?

## Drawing Venn diagrams

**2** A school surveyed 100 students about how they get to school:

- 35 students take the tram (T)
- 68 students take the bus (B)
- 12 students do not take a tram or a bus.

**a)** Complete the Venn diagram to show these results.

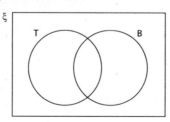

**b)** Work out the probability that a randomly chosen student takes the tram and the bus to school.
Give your answer as a percentage.

........................ %

#  5 Conditional probability

## Using tree diagrams

**Conditional probability** describes the probability of events whose outcomes aren't independent. This is sometimes known as probability without replacement.

Tree diagrams can be used for problems with two or more events. The branches show each event.

> The probability of A given B has occurred is written as P(A | B).

A fruit bowl has three red and four green apples.

Abbie takes an apple at random and eats it, then Ben does the same.

Use a tree diagram to work out the probability that:

a) two red apples are taken

$P(RR) = \frac{3}{7} \times \frac{2}{6} = \frac{6}{42} = \frac{1}{7}$

b) one green apple and one red apple are taken

P(one green, one red) = P(R, G) + P(G, R)

$= \frac{2}{7} + \frac{2}{7} = \frac{4}{7}$

c) at least one green apple is taken.

P(at least one green) = 1 − P(R, R) = $1 - \frac{1}{7} = \frac{6}{7}$

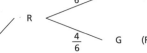
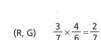

| Abbie | Ben | Outcome | Probability |
|---|---|---|---|

$\frac{3}{7}$ R

$\frac{2}{6}$ R (R, R) $\frac{3}{7} \times \frac{2}{6} = \frac{1}{7}$

$\frac{4}{6}$ G (R, G) $\frac{3}{7} \times \frac{4}{6} = \frac{2}{7}$

$\frac{4}{7}$ G

$\frac{3}{6}$ R (G, R) $\frac{4}{7} \times \frac{3}{6} = \frac{2}{7}$

$\frac{3}{6}$ G (G, G) $\frac{4}{7} \times \frac{3}{6} = \frac{2}{7}$

4 out of the 7 apples are green to begin with. If Abbie takes a green apple, only 3 green apples are left out of 6 in total.

## Using two-way tables and Venn diagrams

Two-way tables and Venn diagrams can also be used for problems with conditional probability.

This two-way table shows the number of part-time and full-time employees working in different departments of a company.

Work out the probability that a randomly chosen employee works:

a) part-time given they work in sales

P(part-time | sales) = $\frac{15}{25} = 0.6$

b) in IT given they are full-time.

P(IT | full-time) = $\frac{25}{50} = \frac{1}{2} = 0.5$

|  |  | Department |  |  |  |
|---|---|---|---|---|---|
|  |  | HR | IT | Sales | Total |
|  | **Part-time** | 25 | 10 | 15 | 50 |
| **Hours** | **Full-time** | 15 | 25 | 10 | 50 |
|  | **Total** | 40 | 35 | 25 | 100 |

There are 25 employees in sales and 15 are part-time.

There are 50 full-time employees, 25 of whom work in IT.

An ice cream shop recorded the toppings ordered by 140 customers.

Use the Venn diagram to work out the probability that a customer ordered sprinkles given they ordered cream. Give your answer to the nearest percent.

Customers ordering cream = 35 + 15 + 5 + 20 = 75

Of those, customers who ordered sprinkles = 15 + 5 = 20

P(S | C) = $\frac{20}{75}$ = 27% (to the nearest %)

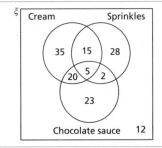

# Conditional probability

## Using tree diagrams

**1** A bag contains marbles. 7 are yellow, 3 are blue and 5 are red.
One marble is taken at random and put to one side. A second marble is then taken at random.

**a)** Use a tree diagram to work out the probability of taking one yellow and one blue marble.

**b)** Work out the probability that **neither** marble is blue.

## Using two-way tables and Venn diagrams

**2** Look at the table of full- and part-time employees on page 128.

Work out the probability that an employee is full-time given that they work in sales. Give your answer as a decimal.

**3** Look at the Venn diagram on page 128.

Work out the probability that a customer ordered all three toppings given that they ordered chocolate sauce. Give your answer as a percentage.

# (6) Handling data

## Collecting data

### The different types of data

| | |
|---|---|
| **Primary data** | Data that you collect |
| **Secondary data** | Data collected by someone else |
| **Discrete data** | Data that can only take certain values in a given range, e.g. the number of goals scored: 0, 1, 2, 3, ... (you can't have half a goal!) |
| **Continuous data** | Data that can have any value within a given range, e.g. the height of a person: 1.83... metres |
| **Numerical data** | Data that is given as numbers, e.g. times to complete a race |
| **Categorical data** | Data that is not numerical, e.g. flavours of ice cream |

### Data collection terms

| | |
|---|---|
| **Survey** | An organised way of collecting data, e.g. by questionnaire or by making observations |
| **Population** | All of the group you are investigating, e.g. the students in a school |
| **Census** | A survey of the entire population |
| **Sample** | A part of the population you are investigating, e.g. 20 students from each year group |
| **Hypothesis** | An idea or assumption which is then tested to decide whether it's true or false, e.g. all students live within a 10-mile radius of a school |

To process and represent data:
- a suitable average (mode, median or mean) and a suitable measure of spread (range or interquartile range) could be calculated
- suitable statistical charts, diagrams or graphs could be drawn.

Results are interpreted and discussed in order to make comparisons and draw conclusions, i.e. decide whether a hypothesis is true, not true or inconclusive.

## Capture–recapture

**Capture–recapture** is a way of estimating the size of a population, e.g. the number of fish in a pond.

**To perform a capture–recapture sample:**
1. Collect a sample and mark each individual, then release them.
2. Collect another sample at a later date and count the number of marked individuals.
3. Work out an estimate for the total population.

The method assumes the ratio of tagged to untagged animals in the second sample is the same as the ratio of tagged to untagged animals in the population.

A scientist wants to estimate the number of fish in a pond. She collects a sample of 50 fish, tags them and releases them. She returns a week later and collects another sample of 50 fish, 5 of which are tagged. Calculate an estimate for the size of the population.

$$\frac{50}{N} = \frac{5}{50}$$ $M = 50$, $R = 5$ and $T = 50$.

$2500 = 5N$

$N = 500$, so there are approximately 500 fish in the pond.

To work out an estimate for the total population: $\frac{M}{N} = \frac{R}{T}$
where $M$ = the total number of marked individuals, $N$ = the total population, $R$ = the number of marked individuals recaptured and $T$ = the total number recaptured.

## Representing data

Ways of representing data include:
- Pie chart (for discrete or categorical data)
- Vertical line graph (for discrete data)
- Bar chart (for discrete or categorical data)
- Histogram (for continuous data, see page 134)
- Time series graph (for data involving change over time, see page 136)
- Frequency polygon
- Stem-and-leaf diagram
- Box plot (see page 134)
- Cumulative frequency diagram (see page 134)
- Scatter graph (see page 136)

Different graphs are suited to different types of data and for making comparisons.

# Handling data

## Collecting data

**1** The owners of a theme park are researching visitor trends.

Write down whether each set of data collected from the theme park is **categorical** or **numerical**. If it is numerical, write down whether it is **discrete** or **continuous**.

**a)** Number of visitors per day .................................................................................

**b)** Heights of the visitors .................................................................................

**c)** Types of food purchased .................................................................................

**d)** Queuing times for attractions .................................................................................

## Capture–recapture

**2** A team of scientists want to estimate the number of orcas in an ocean region. They identify and tag 12 orcas. They return at a later date and identify 10 orcas, two of which are tagged.

Estimate the population of orcas in that ocean region.

.................................................................................

## Representing data

**3** The table gives information about the favourite sport of students in class 11A.

**a)** Draw a pie chart to show this information.

| Favourite sport | Number of students |
|-----------------|--------------------|
| Football | 10 |
| Tennis | 15 |
| Hockey | 12 |
| Rugby | 3 |
| **Total** | |

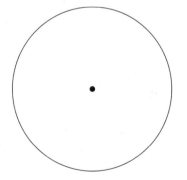

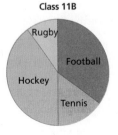

Class 11B

**b)** This pie chart gives information about the favourite sports of students in class 11B.

Katie says there are more students in class 11B than in class 11A who said football was their favourite.

Is she correct? Explain your answer.

.................................................................................

.................................................................................

# Measures of central tendency and spread

## Mode, median, mean and range

An **average** is a measure used to represent a set of data. The most commonly used averages are:
- the **mode**, which is the most common value
- the **median**, which is the middle value of the ordered data
- the **mean** = $\frac{\text{sum of all the values}}{\text{total number of values}}$

Mean, median and mode are **measures of central tendency**. Range and interquartile range are **measures of spread**.

The **range** is the biggest value – smallest value.
The **lower quartile (Q1)** is the value that is one-quarter along the ordered data.
The **upper quartile (Q3)** is the value that is three-quarters along the ordered data.
The **interquartile range (IQR)** is the spread of the inner part of the data; IQR = Q3 – Q1.

For a data set of $n$ values:
- Lower quartile is the $\frac{n+1}{4}$ th value
- Upper quartile is the $\frac{3(n+1)}{4}$ th value.

Use the table below to work out the mode, median, mean, range and interquartile range of the number of pets per family.

| No. of pets ($x$) | Frequency ($f$) |
|---|---|
| 0 | 4 |
| 1 | 7 |
| 2 | 6 |
| 3 | 6 |
| | Total = 23 |

Ordering the data: 0, 0, 0, 0, 1, ①, 1, 1, 1, 1, 1, ②, 2, 2, 2, 2, 2, ③, 3, 3, 3, 3, 3

The circled values in the ordered list are respectively Q1, the median, and Q3.

| $f \times x$ |
|---|
| 0 |
| 7 |
| 12 |
| 18 |
| Total = 37 |

This is the sum of all the data points.

**Mode** is 1 pet per family.
**Median** is the $\frac{23+1}{2}$ = 12th value, which is 2.
**Mean** is $\frac{37}{23}$ = 1.61 pets per family (to 2 d.p.)
**Range** is 3 – 0 = 3

**Lower quartile** is the $\frac{23+1}{4}$ = 6th value, which is 1.
**Upper quartile** is the $\frac{3(23+1)}{4}$ = 18th value, which is 3.
**Interquartile range** is 3 – 1 = 2

## Mode, median and mean from a grouped frequency table

It is not possible to find the exact values from a grouped frequency table, so you can't work out the range. Instead, you can work out the class that contains the mode (the **modal class**) and the class that contains the median. You can also find an estimate of the mean.

**To estimate the mean:**
1. Find the midpoint of the class intervals.
2. Multiply the frequency by the midpoint of each class interval, $f \times x$. Find the total of $f \times x$.
3. Find the total frequency.
4. Estimate the mean using $\frac{\text{sum of } f \times x}{\text{sum of } f}$

The grouped frequency table shows the maximum temperatures for 17 days.

| Recorded temp., $T$ (°C) | Frequency ($f$) |
|---|---|
| $15 \leqslant T < 20$ | 4 |
| $20 \leqslant T < 25$ | 5 |
| $25 \leqslant T < 30$ | 8 |
| | Total = 17 |

a) Write the modal class.
   $25°C \leqslant T < 30°C$ — The class with highest frequency.

b) Write the class that contains the median.
   $20°C \leqslant T < 25°C$ — There are 17 values, so the median is the 9th value, which is in $20°C \leqslant T < 25°C$.

c) Calculate an estimate for the mean of the maximum temperatures.

| Midpoint ($x$) | $fx$ |
|---|---|
| 17.5 | 4 × 17.5 = 70 |
| 22.5 | 5 × 22.5 = 112.5 |
| 27.5 | 8 × 27.5 = 220 |
| | Total = 402.5 |

These are halfway values for the class intervals.

Estimate of the mean = $\frac{\text{sum of } f \times x}{\text{sum of } f}$
$= \frac{402.5}{17}$
$= 23.7°C$ (to 1 d.p.)

# Measures of central tendency and spread

## Mode, median, mean and range

**1** Work out the following for this set of data, giving your answers to 2 decimal places where necessary. You may wish to add columns to the table to help you.

| $x$ | Frequency, $f$ |
|---|---|
| 3 | 1 |
| 4 | 9 |
| 5 | 6 |
| 6 | 3 |

**a)** Mode

**b)** Mean

**c)** Median

**d)** Lower quartile

**e)** Upper quartile

**f)** Interquartile range

**g)** Range

## Mode, median and mean from a grouped frequency table

**2** Work out the following for this set of data, giving your answers to 2 decimal places where necessary. You may wish to add columns to the table to help you..

| Class | Frequency, $f$ |
|---|---|
| $0 < x \leqslant 2$ | 10 |
| $2 < x \leqslant 4$ | 21 |
| $4 < x \leqslant 6$ | 13 |
| $6 < x \leqslant 8$ | 7 |

**a)** The modal class

**b)** Class that contains the median

**c)** An estimate of the mean

# Histograms and cumulative frequency diagrams

## Histograms

A **histogram** is used to show continuous data. The area of each bar represents the frequency.

Area of bar (frequency of class interval) = frequency density × width of class interval

frequency density = $\dfrac{\text{frequency of class interval}}{\text{width of class interval}}$

*Frequency **D**ensity = Frequency **D**ivided by class width*

**To draw a histogram with unequal class widths:**

1. Work out the class width.
2. Divide the frequency by the class width to find the frequency density.

Draw bars using the class intervals and frequency densities. The bars should be touching.

> The bar height represents the frequency density.

The table below shows data for the ages of some cinemagoers. Draw a histogram to represent the data.

| Age, $A$ (years) | Frequency | | Class width | Frequency density |
|---|---|---|---|---|
| $0 < A \leqslant 20$ | 30 | Add columns to record the class width and the frequency density. | 20 | $30 \div 20 = 1.5$ |
| $20 < A \leqslant 30$ | 40 | | 10 | $40 \div 10 = 4$ |
| $30 < A \leqslant 40$ | 50 | | 10 | $50 \div 10 = 5$ |
| $40 < A \leqslant 60$ | 60 | | 20 | $60 \div 20 = 3$ |
| $60 < A \leqslant 100$ | 20 | | 40 | $20 \div 40 = 0.5$ |

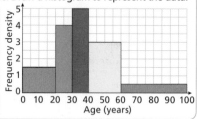

## Cumulative frequency diagrams

**To draw a cumulative frequency diagram:**

1. Work out the running totals of the frequencies.
2. Plot these totals against the upper class boundaries.
3. Join the points with either straight lines or a curve.

A cumulative frequency graph can be used to find:
- the median of the data: read off from halfway up the total frequency
- the lower and upper quartiles: read off from one-quarter and three-quarters of the total frequency
- the proportion or amount of the data that is above or below a particular value.

The table shows the time taken for 60 students to travel to school. The shortest time was 2 minutes and the longest time was 50 minutes.

| Time taken, $T$ (minutes) | Frequency |
|---|---|
| $2 < T \leqslant 10$ | 3 |
| $10 < T \leqslant 20$ | 7 |
| $20 < T \leqslant 30$ | 14 |
| $30 < T \leqslant 40$ | 24 |
| $40 < T \leqslant 50$ | 12 |

a) Draw a cumulative frequency graph.

| Time taken, $T$ (minutes) | Frequency | Cumulative frequency |
|---|---|---|
| $2 < T \leqslant 10$ | 3 | 3 |
| $10 < T \leqslant 20$ | 7 | $(3 + 7 =) 10$ |
| $20 < T \leqslant 30$ | 14 | $(14 + 10 =) 24$ |
| $30 < T \leqslant 40$ | 24 | $(24 + 24 =) 48$ |
| $40 < T \leqslant 50$ | 12 | $(48 + 12 =) 60$ |

b) Use the cumulative frequency graph to draw a box plot.

c) Estimate the percentage of students who take more than 15 minutes to get to school.

$\dfrac{54}{60} = 90\%$

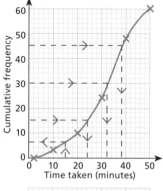

Plot the points against the **upper boundary** of each class: (2, 0), (10, 3), (20, 10), (30, 24), (40, 48), (50, 60)

Read off at 30 for the median (32 minutes), at 15 for the lower quartile (24 minutes), and at 45 for the upper quartile (38 minutes).

6 students take less than 15 minutes, so 54 out of 60 take longer than that.

# Histograms and cumulative frequency diagrams

## Histograms

**1** The table shows the ages of visitors at a theme park.

Draw a histogram to show the data.

| Age, $A$ (years) | Number of visitors | Class width | Frequency density |
|---|---|---|---|
| $0 < A \leqslant 10$ | 1480 | | |
| $10 < A \leqslant 30$ | 2100 | | |
| $30 < A \leqslant 50$ | 1620 | | |
| $50 < A \leqslant 90$ | 800 | | |

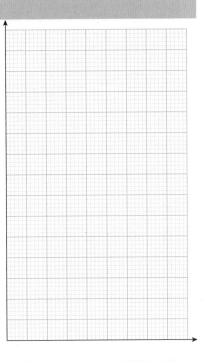

## Cumulative frequency diagrams

**2** This cumulative frequency diagram shows the ages of visitors at the theme park.

Use the diagram to work out:

**a)** the median age of visitors

.................................................

**b)** the interquartile range of visitors

.................................................

**c)** the percentage of visitors who are under the age of 20, giving your answer to the nearest percent.

.................................................%

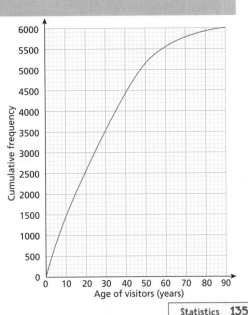

# 6 Scatter graphs and time series

## Scatter graphs

A **scatter graph** helps to compare two sets of data on the same pair of axes. **Correlation** describes any trend shown.

> Correlation means the two values share some sort of relationship; it does not mean that one value causes the other. Correlation is not causation.

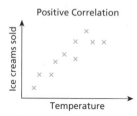

Positive Correlation

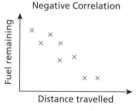

Negative Correlation

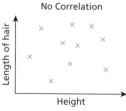

No Correlation

A **line of best fit** is a straight line that shows the trend of the data, but it doesn't have to pass exactly through any of the points. It can be used to estimate unknown values **within** the range of the points plotted. Correlation is 'strong' if all points lie very close to the line of best fit and 'weak' if they are more spread.

The table shows how much money a company spent on advertising and the revenue generated.

| Advertising spend (£k) | 10 | 15 | 20 | 25 | 30 | 35 | 40 | 45 | 55 |
|---|---|---|---|---|---|---|---|---|---|
| Revenue generated (£k) | 50 | 70 | 75 | 90 | 130 | 160 | 50 | 180 | 220 |

a) Draw a scatter graph to show the data.

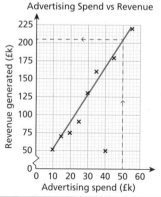

b) What type of correlation is shown?

> As the advertising spend increases, the revenue generated increases.

The graph shows a positive correlation.

c) Estimate the revenue generated if the company spends £50 000 on advertising.

> Add a line of best fit (shown by the red line) and use it for estimation (shown by the dashed line).

If the company spends £50 000, it will generate approximately £205 000 in revenue.

d) Identify the outlier in this data.

> Outliers are any points that do not fit the trend.

The data point (40, 50) is the outlier.

## Time series graphs

A **time series graph** (a **line graph**) can be used for discrete or continuous data to show change over time.

The table shows data about temperatures at different times of the day.

| Time | 10 am | 11 am | Noon | 1 pm | 2 pm |
|---|---|---|---|---|---|
| Temp. (°C) | 11°C | 12°C | 13°C | 14°C | 12°C |

Draw a time series graph to show the data.

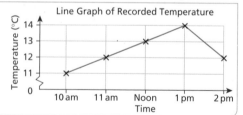

# Scatter graphs and time series

## Scatter graphs

**1** The scatter graph shows the maximum daily temperature and the number of ice creams sold at a park over a period of 14 days.

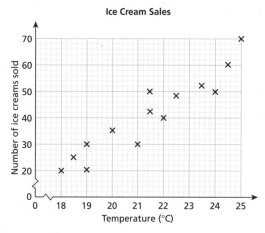

**Ice Cream Sales**

**a)** Draw a line of best fit on the graph.

**b)** Use the line of best fit to estimate the number of ice creams sold if the temperature is 23°C.

## Time series graphs

**2** The number of ice creams sold each day for a week at another park was recorded in this table.

| Day | Mon | Tue | Wed | Thu | Fri | Sat | Sun |
|---|---|---|---|---|---|---|---|
| Ice creams sold | 10 | 15 | 8 | 12 | 27 | 38 | 34 |

Draw a time series graph to show the data.

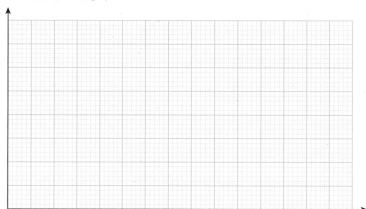

# Mixed questions

## Non-calculator questions

**1** Work out the equation of the line that is perpendicular to the line $y = 3x - 2$ and passes through the point $(0, 4)$.

........................................

**2** **a)** Solve     $8(1 + 4x) - 4(x + 3) = 0$

$x =$ ........................

**b)** Solve     $\frac{y}{2} - 5 = 11$

$y =$ ........................

**c)** Factorise $2x^2 - 5x - 3$ and hence solve $2x^2 = 5x + 3$

$x =$ ................... or $x =$ ...................

**3** The box plots show information about the midday temperatures for two towns in September.

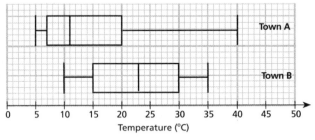

Compare the temperatures in town A and town B.

........................................................................................................................................

........................................................................................................................................

........................................................................................................................................

........................................................................................................................................

**4** Write down the exact value of:

**a)** $8^{\frac{1}{3}} =$ ........................     **b)** $9^{-2} =$ ........................     **c)** $125^{-\frac{2}{3}} =$ ........................

**5** When driving to the shops, I go through two sets of traffic lights. The probability that I stop at the first set is $\frac{1}{4}$. The probability that I stop at the second set is $\frac{2}{3}$.

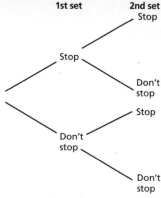

1st set      2nd set

**a)** Complete the tree diagram to show the possible outcomes when going through the two sets of lights.

**b)** Work out the probability that I am stopped by **at least one** set of traffic lights.

**6** Shape A is shown on the coordinate grid.

**a)** Reflect shape A in the line $y = -1$.
Label the image as shape B.

**b)** Translate shape B by the vector $\begin{pmatrix} -5 \\ 1 \end{pmatrix}$.
Label the image as shape C.

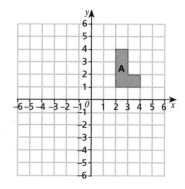

**7** Jack has £5 more than Kyle.
Kyle has half as much as Liam.
Liam has £$x$.
Jack and Kyle give their money to Liam. Liam now has £20.

**a)** Show that $x + \frac{x}{2} + \frac{x}{2} + 5 = 20$

**b)** How much money did Liam have to start with?

£ .................................

# Mixed questions

## Calculator allowed questions

**8** Mateo is buying a new refrigerator and sees offers from three shops.

FRIDGE WORLD

$\frac{1}{3}$ off usual price of
**£810**

FRIDGE BARGAINS

██ PAY DEPOSIT OF £100 ██
Then pay 12 equal
instalments of £40

The Electric Store

**£500**
plus
**20% VAT**

Mateo wants to pay as little as possible.

From which shop should he buy the refrigerator? Show your working.

**9** In an electrical circuit, the current, $I$, is inversely proportional to the resistance, $R$.
When $I = 10$ amps (A), $R = 24$ ohms (Ω).

**a)** Work out the equation of proportionality.

**b)** Explain what happens to the current when the resistance doubles.

**10** Abby and Jude share £84 in the ratio 7 : 5.

Abby says that she gets £15 more than Jude.
Is she correct? You must show your working.

# Mixed questions

**11** A, B and D are points on the circumference of the circle.

Triangle BCD is isosceles.

Work out the size of angle $x$.
Give reasons for your answer.

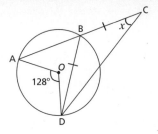

$x =$ ................................ °

................................................................................................................................

................................................................................................................................

**12 a)** Write $(3 + \sqrt{5})^2$ in the form $a + b\sqrt{5}$.

................................................

**b)** Rationalise the denominator and simplify $\frac{10}{\sqrt{2}}$

................................................

**13** The diagram shows a solid metal cylinder
and an open cuboid.

The cylinder is melted down and the
metal is poured into the cuboid.

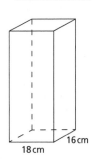

Work out the height of the metal in the cuboid. Give your answer to the nearest centimetre.

................................ cm

# Mixed questions

**14** Work out the size of the smallest angle in this triangle.

C

7 cm

5 cm

A

6 cm

B

.................................. °

**15** The $n$th term of a sequence is $n^2 + 5$.

**a)** Work out the 6th term of the sequence.

.................................................

**b)** Is the number 125 in the sequence? Give reasons for your answer.

.................................................................................................

.................................................................................................

**16** The rectangle has an area of 27 cm².

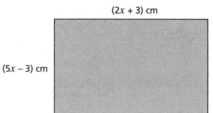

(2x + 3) cm

(5x – 3) cm

**a)** Show that $10x^2 + 9x - 36 = 0$

.................................................................................................

.................................................................................................

.................................................................................................

**b)** Use the quadratic formula to solve the equation $10x^2 + 9x - 36 = 0$

$x = $ .................... or $x = $ ....................

**c)** Work out the length of the longest side of the rectangle.

.................................... cm

# Mixed questions

**17** The table shows the masses of 240 parcels collected by a courier.

**a)** Draw a fully labelled histogram to show this information.

| Mass, $m$ (grams) | Frequency |
|---|---|
| $0 < m \leqslant 100$ | 40 |
| $100 < m \leqslant 300$ | 64 |
| $300 < m \leqslant 500$ | 86 |
| $500 < m \leqslant 1000$ | 50 |

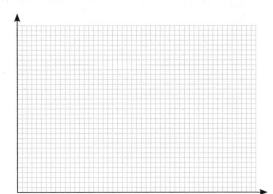

**b)** The next day, the courier collected 500 parcels.

Use the data in the table to estimate the number of parcels that weighed 100 grams or less.

........................................

**18** Work out the sizes of angles $x$ and $y$. Give reasons for your answers.

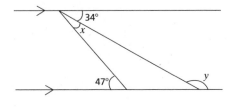

$x =$ ...................... $^{\circ}$

...................................................................................................
...................................................................................................
...................................................................................................

$y =$ ...................... $^{\circ}$

...................................................................................................
...................................................................................................
...................................................................................................

# Mixed questions

**19** OABC is a parallelogram.
$\overrightarrow{OA} = \mathbf{a}$ and $\overrightarrow{OC} = \mathbf{c}$.

X is the midpoint of the line AC.

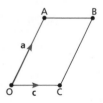

**a)** Express the position of X in terms of vectors **a** and **c**.

$$\overrightarrow{OX} = \text{..........................}$$

**b)** Point D is a point outside the parallelogram such that point X divides $\overrightarrow{OD}$ in the ratio 1 : 2.
Express the position of point D in terms of vectors **a** and **c**.

$$\overrightarrow{OD} = \text{..........................}$$

**c)** Express the position of B in terms of vectors **a** and **c**.
What can you say about point B?

..............................................................................................................................................

..............................................................................................................................................

**20** You are given the quadratic function $y = x^2 + 6x + 5$

**a)** Work out the $x$-intercepts.

$$x = \text{............} \text{ and } x = \text{............}$$

**b)** Work out the turning point.

.......................................................

**c)** Hence, draw the graph of $y = x^2 + 6x + 5$

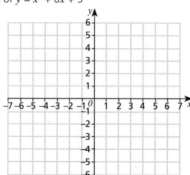

# Key facts and vocabulary

## Number

| | | |
|---|---|---|
| **Calculations in standard form** | To calculate in standard form:<br>**1.** Change the numbers to ordinary form.<br>**2.** Complete the calculation.<br>**3.** Change the numbers back to standard form if required. | $(1.328 \times 10^3) + (2.7 \times 10^2) =$<br>$1.328 \times 10^3 = 1328$<br>$2.7 \times 10^2 = 270$<br>$1328 + 270 = 1598$<br>$1598 = 1.598 \times 10^3$ |
| **Multiplying and dividing fractions** | To multiply fractions, multiply the numerators together and multiply the denominators together.<br>To divide fractions, remember KFC. | Keep the first fraction as it is<br>Flip the second fraction<br>Change $\div$ to $\times$ |
| **Multiplying and dividing negative numbers** | $\oplus \times \oplus = \oplus$  $\ominus \times \oplus = \ominus$<br>$\ominus \times \ominus = \oplus$  $\oplus \times \ominus = \ominus$ | $\oplus \div \oplus = \oplus$  $\ominus \div \oplus = \ominus$<br>$\ominus \div \ominus = \oplus$  $\oplus \div \ominus = \ominus$ |
| **Order of operations** | **B I D M A S**<br>( ) $x^2$ $\div$ or $\times$ $+$ or $-$ | |
| **Prime factor decomposition** | A process for breaking down a number into its prime factors. | 90 ⟨9, 10⟩ 9⟨3,3⟩ 10⟨2,5⟩   $90 = 2 \times 3^2 \times 5$ |
| **Rationalising the denominator** | Turning the denominator into a rational number.<br>$\frac{10}{\sqrt{5}} = \frac{10}{\sqrt{5}} \times \frac{\sqrt{5}}{\sqrt{5}} = \frac{10\sqrt{5}}{5} = 2\sqrt{5}$ | |
| **Surd** | A root that cannot be simplified to a rational number, e.g. $\sqrt{2}$.<br>Rules for simplifying and calculating with surds:<br>$\sqrt{a \times b} = \sqrt{a} \times \sqrt{b}$  $\sqrt{a} \times \sqrt{a} = a$  $\sqrt{\frac{a}{b}} = \frac{\sqrt{a}}{\sqrt{b}}$ (or $\sqrt{a} \div \sqrt{b}$) | |

## Algebra

| | |
|---|---|
| **Arithmetic sequence** | Terms go up or down by the same amount (common difference) each time.<br>2, 5, 8, 11, 14, ...  Common difference $+3$<br>5, 3, 1, –1, –3, ...  Common difference $-2$ |
| **Composite function** | A combination of functions, written as $fg(x)$.    Given $f(x) = 2x$ and $g(x) = x^2 + 3$,<br>$fg(x) = 2(x^2 + 3) = 2x^2 + 6$ |
| **Completing the square** | **1.** Rearrange the expression to the form $x^2 + bx + c$.<br>**2.** Divide the $b$ term by 2 and write the expression as $(x + \frac{b}{2})^2 - (\frac{b}{2})^2 + c$.<br>**3.** Simplify.    Solving an equation by completing the square:<br>$x^2 - 6x - 1 = 0$<br>$(x - 3)^2 - 3^2 - 1 = 0$<br>$(x - 3)^2 = 10$<br>$x = 3 \pm \sqrt{10}$ |
| **Cubic functions** | Cubic functions have an $x^3$ term as the highest power of $x$, e.g. $y = x^3$ or $y = x^3 - 4$.<br>The general shape of a cubic function is: 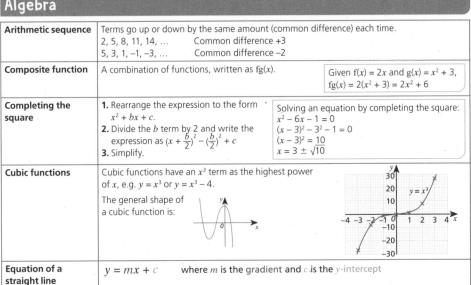 |
| **Equation of a straight line** | $y = mx + c$    where $m$ is the gradient and $c$ is the $y$-intercept |

# Key facts and vocabulary

| Expanding or multiplying out two sets of brackets | Multiply every term in the first bracket by every term in the second bracket. |
|---|---|

Grid method

$(2x + 3)(x - 4)$

|  | $2x$ | $+3$ |
|---|---|---|
| $x$ | $2x^2$ | $3x$ |
| $-4$ | $-8x$ | $-12$ |

$= 2x^2 - 5x - 12$

FOIL method

Firsts ⌢ Lasts

$(a + b)(c + d)$

Inners

Outers

| Factorising | Writing an expression as a multiplication using the highest common factor and brackets, e.g. $8xy - 6x^2 = 2x(4y - 3x)$ |
|---|---|

| Working out the equation of a line | 1. Find two points on the line. <br> 2. Work out the gradient between them. <br> 3. Find the $y$-intercept. <br> 4. Write the equation using $y = mx + c$. |
|---|---|

$m = \frac{y_2 - y_1}{x_2 - x_1}$

$m = \frac{7 - 5}{2 - 1} = 2$

$y$-intercept is 3

Equation is $y = 2x + 3$

| Geometric sequence | Each term is multiplied by the same number to get the next term. <br> 2, 4, 8, 16, 32, ...  Each term is multiplied by 2 <br> 1000, 100, 10, 1, 0.1, ...  Each term is multiplied by 0.1 |
|---|---|

| Inverse function | Links the output of a function back to the input, written as $f^{-1}(x)$. <br> To work out the inverse of a function:  1. Write $f(x)$ as $y$. <br> 2. Swap the $x$ and $y$ in the equation. <br> 3. Solve for $y$. <br> 4. Write $f(x)$ for $y$. |
|---|---|

| Laws of indices | To multiply powers of the same base, add the powers | $a^m \times a^n = a^{(m+n)}$ |
|---|---|---|
|  | To divide powers of the same base, subtract the powers | $a^m \div a^n = a^{(m-n)}$ |
|  | To raise a power to another power, multiply the powers | $(a^m)^n = a^{(m \times n)}$ |
|  | Any base to the power of 1 is itself | $a^1 = a$ |
|  | Any base to the power of 0 is 1 | $a^0 = 1$ |
|  | A negative power means the reciprocal of the power | $a^{-m} = \frac{1}{a^m}$ |

| Midpoint of a line segment | Midpoint $= \left(\frac{x_1 + x_2}{2}, \frac{y_1 + y_2}{2}\right)$ <br> To work out the midpoint of the line segment shown: <br> Midpoint $= \left(\frac{3 + (-1)}{2}, \frac{1 + 3}{2}\right)$ <br> $= (1, 2)$ |
|---|---|

$(-1, 3)$   $(3, 1)$

| Quadratic formula | Used to solve a quadratic equation of the form $ax^2 + bx + c = 0$ | $x = \frac{-b \pm \sqrt{b^2 - 4ac}}{2a}$ |
|---|---|---|

| Quadratic functions | Quadratic functions (or equations) have an $x^2$ term as the highest power of $x$. <br><br> Quadratic graphs are symmetrical, U-shaped curves. If they have a positive $x^2$ term, they open upwards $\cup$. If they have a negative $x^2$ term, they open downwards $\cap$. |
|---|---|

y-intercept

x-intercepts (roots)

Turning point

# Key facts and vocabulary

| | |
|---|---|
| **Simplifying expressions** | Combining like terms in an expression, e.g. $\widehat{(3x)} + \widehat{(2y)} + \widehat{(2x)} + 2x^2 - \widehat{(3y)} = 2x^2 + \widehat{(5x)} - \widehat{(y)}$ |
| **Solving an equation** | Working out the value of the unknown. Use inverse operations to get all the $x$ terms on one side and all the numbers on the other.<br><br>To solve an equation with brackets, expand the brackets first.<br><br>To solve an equation with fractions, 'undo' the fractions by multiplying both sides by the denominator. |
| **Solving quadratic equations by factorising** | 1. Rearrange so the equation is equal to zero.<br>2. Factorise.<br>3. Set each bracket equal to zero.<br>4. Solve. $\begin{aligned} 2x^2 + 15x &= -7 \\ 2x^2 + 15x + 7 &= 0 \\ (2x + 1)(x + 7) &= 0 \\ 2x + 1 = 0 \text{ or } x + 7 &= 0 \\ x = -\frac{1}{2} \text{ or } x &= -7 \end{aligned}$ <br><br>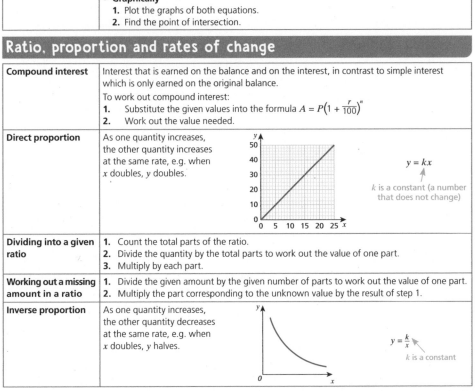 |
| **Solving simultaneous equations** | Three methods:<br>• **Substitution**<br>  1. Write one equation so that one variable is isolated.<br>  2. Substitute into the second equation and solve.<br>• **Elimination**<br>  1. Multiply or divide the equations to make the coefficient of one variable the same.<br>  2. Add or subtract the new equations to remove the variable.<br>  3. Solve.<br>• **Graphically**<br>  1. Plot the graphs of both equations.<br>  2. Find the point of intersection. |

## Ratio, proportion and rates of change

| | |
|---|---|
| **Compound interest** | Interest that is earned on the balance and on the interest, in contrast to simple interest which is only earned on the original balance.<br><br>To work out compound interest:<br>1. Substitute the given values into the formula $A = P\left(1 + \frac{r}{100}\right)^n$<br>2. Work out the value needed. |
| **Direct proportion** | As one quantity increases, the other quantity increases at the same rate, e.g. when $x$ doubles, $y$ doubles. $\qquad y = kx$ <br><br>$k$ is a constant (a number that does not change) |
| **Dividing into a given ratio** | 1. Count the total parts of the ratio.<br>2. Divide the quantity by the total parts to work out the value of one part.<br>3. Multiply by each part. |
| **Working out a missing amount in a ratio** | 1. Divide the given amount by the given number of parts to work out the value of one part.<br>2. Multiply the part corresponding to the unknown value by the result of step 1. |
| **Inverse proportion** | As one quantity increases, the other quantity decreases at the same rate, e.g. when $x$ doubles, $y$ halves. $\qquad y = \frac{k}{x}$ <br><br>$k$ is a constant |

# Key facts and vocabulary

| Multiplier | The decimal value used to work out a percentage change.<br>To increase by 20%, the multiplier is 1.2<br>To decrease by 20%, the multiplier is 0.8 |
|---|---|
| Percentage change | Percentage change = $\frac{\text{amount of increase or decrease}}{\text{original value}} \times 100\%$<br>Repeated percentage change:<br>New value = original value $\times$ multiplier$^x$ (where $x$ is the number of changes) |
| Reverse percentages | Working backwards to find the original amount.<br>Divide by the multiplier. |
| Unit ratio | A ratio written in the form $1 : n$ or $n : 1$. It can be used to compare ratios. |

## Geometry and measures

| Arc | Part of the circumference of a circle.<br>Length of an arc = $\frac{\text{angle at centre}}{360°} \times$ circumference of circle<br><br>Circumference $\rightarrow$     Arc |
|---|---|
| Area of a circle | $A = \pi r^2$ |
| Area of a trapezium | $A = \frac{1}{2}(a + b)h$ |
| Area rule | Used to work out the area of a triangle when you know two sides and the angle between them.<br>$A = \frac{1}{2}\, ab \sin C$ |
| Bearing | A three-digit angle measurement to show the direction of one place to another, starting North and measuring clockwise, e.g. 030°, 120°, 348°. |
| Congruent | Congruent shapes are exactly the same shape and size.<br>Two triangles are congruent if one or more of these four criteria are true: |

| Side, Side, Side (SSS) | Side, Angle, Side (SAS) | Angle, Side, Angle (ASA) or Angle, Angle, Side (AAS) | Right angle, Hypotenuse, Side (RHS) |
|---|---|---|---|

| Enlargement | An enlargement multiplies:<br>• each length on the shape by the scale factor<br>• the distance from the centre by the scale factor.<br>To describe an enlargement:<br>Enlargement scale factor ................, centre ................<br>                number         point<br>An enlargement by a negative scale factor creates an upside-down image that is on the opposite side of the centre of enlargement. |
|---|---|

# Key facts and vocabulary

| | |
|---|---|
| **Exterior and interior angles** | Sum of interior angles in a polygon = (number of sides − 2) × 180°<br>Sum of exterior angles in a polygon = 360°<br>Interior angle + exterior angle = 180°<br><br>Exterior angle    Interior angle |
| **Locus** (plural: **loci**) | The set of points that satisfy a given condition or a set of conditions. For example, the bisector of an angle is the locus of points that are equidistant from the two sides of the angle. |
| **Pythagoras' theorem** | $a^2 + b^2 = c^2$<br><br>$c$ is the length of the hypotenuse<br><br>$a$ and $b$ are the lengths of the two shorter sides |
| **Rotation** | A rotation turns a shape around a point, called the centre of rotation.<br>Use tracing paper.<br>To describe a rotation:<br>Rotation ..............° clockwise/anticlockwise, centre ..............<br>    angle        direction        point |
| **Scale factor** | The value by which all side lengths are multiplied in an enlargement.<br><br>A to B: enlargement scale factor 2<br>B to A: enlargement scale factor $\frac{1}{2}$<br><br>2 × 2   A   B   $6 \times \frac{1}{2}$ |
| **Sector** | The area of a circle enclosed by two radii and the arc between them. |
| **Similar** | Similar shapes are enlargements of each other:<br>• The angles in each shape are the same.<br>• They have the same shape but different sizes.<br>• Each side length in the enlarged shape has been multiplied by the same scale factor.<br><br>X   Y |
| **Sine and cosine rules** | Used to work out missing sides and angles in non-right-angled triangles.<br>Sine rule: $\frac{a}{\sin A} = \frac{b}{\sin B} = \frac{c}{\sin C}$ or $\frac{\sin A}{a} = \frac{\sin B}{b} = \frac{\sin C}{c}$<br>Cosine rule: $a^2 = b^2 + c^2 - 2bc \cos A$<br>or $\cos A = \frac{b^2 + c^2 - a^2}{2bc}$ |
| **Translation** | A translation slides a shape across a grid.<br>Translation 4 squares right, 2 down.<br>To describe a translation, a column vector can be used:<br><br>$\begin{pmatrix} 4 \\ -2 \end{pmatrix}$ ← Movement right/left (a negative value means 'left')<br>← Movement up/down (a negative value means 'down')<br><br>Object   Image |

# Key facts and vocabulary

| | |
|---|---|
| **Trigonometric ratios** | $\sin \theta = \dfrac{\text{opposite}}{\text{hypotenuse}} = \dfrac{\text{opp}}{\text{hyp}}$ <br><br> $\cos \theta = \dfrac{\text{adjacent}}{\text{hypotenuse}} = \dfrac{\text{adj}}{\text{hyp}}$ <br><br> $\tan \theta = \dfrac{\text{opposite}}{\text{adjacent}} = \dfrac{\text{opp}}{\text{adj}}$ <br><br> You can remember these using: <br>      **S O H**     **C A H**     **T O A** <br> $\sin = \dfrac{\text{opp}}{\text{hyp}}$     $\cos = \dfrac{\text{adj}}{\text{hyp}}$     $\tan = \dfrac{\text{opp}}{\text{adj}}$ |
| **Vector** | A line segment of a certain length and a particular direction. <br><br> Vector $\overrightarrow{AB} = \mathbf{a} = \begin{pmatrix} 3 \\ -4 \end{pmatrix}$ |
| **Volume of a prism** | Volume of a prism = area of cross-section × length, where the cross-section is the 2D shape made when cutting through the prism |

## Probability

| | |
|---|---|
| **Conditional probability** | The probability of events whose outcomes are dependent on another event. Venn diagrams and tree diagrams are useful ways of calculating conditional probability. |
| **Expected result** | Expected result = P(event) × number of trials <br> For rolling a dice 30 times, expected number of 3s = $\frac{1}{6} \times 30 = 5$ |
| **Independent events** | The result of one event does not change the probability of the second event, e.g. for a dice, rolling a 6 does not change the probability of rolling a 6 next time. |
| **Mutually exclusive** | Two events that cannot occur at the same time. <br> The probabilities of all the mutually exclusive events in a trial add up to 1. <br> For this spinner, P(Y) + P(G) + P(R) + P(B) = 1 |
| **Outcome** | The result of a probability experiment or trial, e.g. for the experiment 'rolling a dice', possible outcomes are 1, 2, 3, 4, 5 or 6. |
| **Probability of an event** | $P(\text{event}) = \dfrac{\text{number of ways the outcome can occur}}{\text{total number of possible outcomes}}$ <br><br> For this spinner, $P(R) = \frac{1}{4}$ |
| **Probability of an event not happening** | P(event not happening) = 1 − P(event happening) <br> For this spinner, P(not blue) = 1 − P(blue) |
| **Probability of combined independent events** | The product rule of independent events is P(A and B) = P(A) × P(B) |

# Key facts and vocabulary

| | |
|---|---|
| **Relative frequency** | Relative frequency = $\dfrac{\text{number of times the event occurred}}{\text{total number of trials}}$ <br><br> The greater the number of trials, the closer the relative frequency gets to the theoretical probability. |
| **Theoretical probability** | Probability you calculate using this formula: <br><br> P(event) = $\dfrac{\text{number of ways the outcome can occur}}{\text{total number of possible outcomes}}$ |
| **Tree diagram** | To work out the probability of combined events, multiply the probability of the outcomes along each branch. <br><br> The probabilities on each pair of branches should sum to 1. <br><br> 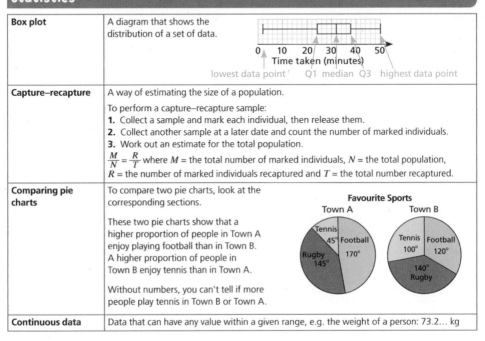 0.3 — School dinner — 0.3 — School dinner P(SS) = 0.3 × 0.3 = 0.09; 0.7 — Packed lunch P(SP) = 0.3 × 0.7 = 0.21; 0.7 — Packed lunch — 0.3 — School dinner P(PS) = 0.3 × 0.7 = 0.21; 0.7 — Packed lunch P(PP) = 0.7 × 0.7 = 0.49 |
| **Venn diagram** | A diagram showing the relationship between two or more things. <br><br> This Venn diagram shows whether students had cereal, eggs, both, or neither for breakfast. <br><br> ξ  Cereal  Eggs  12  3  8  2 |

## Statistics

| | |
|---|---|
| **Box plot** | A diagram that shows the distribution of a set of data. <br><br> 0  10  20  30  40  50 <br> Time taken (minutes) <br> lowest data point   Q1 median Q3  highest data point |
| **Capture–recapture** | A way of estimating the size of a population. <br><br> To perform a capture–recapture sample: <br> **1.** Collect a sample and mark each individual, then release them. <br> **2.** Collect another sample at a later date and count the number of marked individuals. <br> **3.** Work out an estimate for the total population. <br><br> $\dfrac{M}{N} = \dfrac{R}{T}$ where $M$ = the total number of marked individuals, $N$ = the total population, $R$ = the number of marked individuals recaptured and $T$ = the total number recaptured. |
| **Comparing pie charts** | To compare two pie charts, look at the corresponding sections. <br><br> These two pie charts show that a higher proportion of people in Town A enjoy playing football than in Town B. A higher proportion of people in Town B enjoy tennis than in Town A. <br><br> Without numbers, you can't tell if more people play tennis in Town B or Town A. <br><br> **Favourite Sports** <br> Town A: Tennis 45°, Football 170°, Rugby 145° <br> Town B: Tennis 100°, Football 120°, Rugby 140° |
| **Continuous data** | Data that can have any value within a given range, e.g. the weight of a person: 73.2... kg |

# Key facts and vocabulary

| | |
|---|---|
| **Cumulative frequency diagram** | Shows the cumulative frequency (running total) of a set of data. 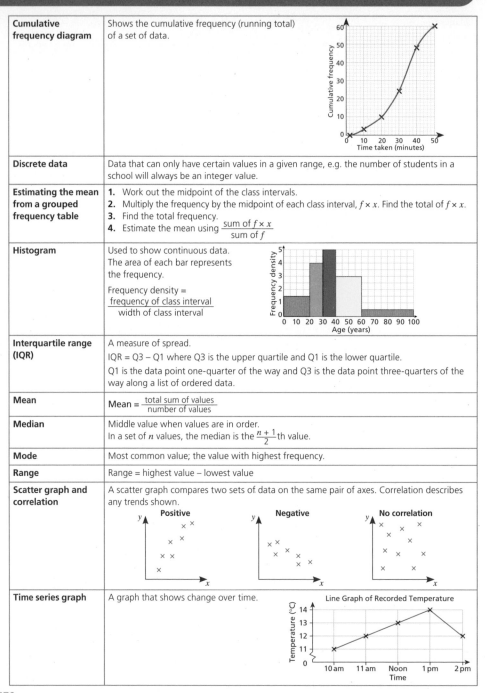 |
| **Discrete data** | Data that can only have certain values in a given range, e.g. the number of students in a school will always be an integer value. |
| **Estimating the mean from a grouped frequency table** | 1. Work out the midpoint of the class intervals.<br>2. Multiply the frequency by the midpoint of each class interval, $f \times x$. Find the total of $f \times x$.<br>3. Find the total frequency.<br>4. Estimate the mean using $\dfrac{\text{sum of } f \times x}{\text{sum of } f}$ |
| **Histogram** | Used to show continuous data.<br>The area of each bar represents the frequency.<br><br>Frequency density = $\dfrac{\text{frequency of class interval}}{\text{width of class interval}}$ |
| **Interquartile range (IQR)** | A measure of spread.<br>IQR = Q3 – Q1 where Q3 is the upper quartile and Q1 is the lower quartile.<br>Q1 is the data point one-quarter of the way and Q3 is the data point three-quarters of the way along a list of ordered data. |
| **Mean** | Mean = $\dfrac{\text{total sum of values}}{\text{number of values}}$ |
| **Median** | Middle value when values are in order.<br>In a set of $n$ values, the median is the $\dfrac{n+1}{2}$th value. |
| **Mode** | Most common value; the value with highest frequency. |
| **Range** | Range = highest value – lowest value |
| **Scatter graph and correlation** | A scatter graph compares two sets of data on the same pair of axes. Correlation describes any trends shown. |
| **Time series graph** | A graph that shows change over time. |

# Answers

## Page 7
1. a) 781    b) 1835    c) 82    d) 1246
2. a) 16 170    b) 1246    c) 9361    d) 1833
3. a) 82    b) 283    c) 53    d) 220.5

## Page 9
1. a) $3\frac{1}{3} + 4\frac{3}{4} = 3 + 4 + \frac{4}{12} + \frac{9}{12} = 7 + \frac{13}{12} = 8\frac{1}{12}$
   b) $2\frac{3}{8} + 1\frac{1}{2} = 2 + 1 + \frac{3}{8} + \frac{4}{8} = 3\frac{7}{8}$
   c) $3\frac{1}{2} - 2\frac{1}{3} = \frac{7}{2} - \frac{7}{3} = \frac{21}{6} - \frac{14}{6} = \frac{7}{6} = 1\frac{1}{6}$
   d) $5\frac{2}{3} - 3\frac{1}{8} = 5 - 3 + \frac{2}{3} - \frac{1}{8} = 2 + \frac{16}{24} - \frac{3}{24} = 2\frac{13}{24}$
2. a) $2\frac{1}{3} \times 3\frac{3}{4} = \frac{7}{3} \times \frac{15}{4} = \frac{105}{12} = 8\frac{9}{12} = 8\frac{3}{4}$
   b) $1\frac{3}{8} \times 2\frac{1}{4} = \frac{11}{8} \times \frac{9}{4} = \frac{99}{32} = 3\frac{3}{32}$
3. a) $2\frac{2}{5} \div 1\frac{1}{8} = \frac{12}{5} \div \frac{9}{8} = \frac{12}{5} \times \frac{8}{9} = \frac{32}{15} = 2\frac{2}{15}$
   b) $3\frac{3}{4} \div \frac{2}{3} = \frac{15}{4} \times \frac{3}{2} = \frac{45}{8} = 5\frac{5}{8}$
4. a) 1 m = 100 cm, so $\frac{15}{100} = \frac{3}{20}$
   b) 1 g = 1000 mg, so $\frac{30}{15000} = \frac{1}{500}$
5. $1 - \frac{3}{5} = \frac{2}{5}$ of the students took packed lunch.
   $\frac{2}{5} \times 30 = (30 \div 5) \times 2 = 12$

## Page 11
1. 0.588, 0.805, 0.85, 8.05, 8.5
2. a) 20.29    b) 53.28
3. a) 47.12    b) 38.221
4. a) 7.1    b) 96
5. a) $0.512 = \frac{512}{1000} = \frac{64}{125}$
   b) $\frac{5}{8} = 5 \div 8 = 0.625$

## Page 13
1. a) 60    b) 15
2. a) 8    b) 4
3. a) $2 \times 2 \times 2 \times 2 \times 2 = 2^5$
   b) $2 \times 2 \times 2 \times 5 = 2^3 \times 5$
4. a) There are three 2s in common
   so HCF = $2 \times 2 \times 2 = 8$
   b) There are two 2s and one 5 left
   so LCM = $8 \times 2 \times 2 \times 5 = 160$

## Page 15
1. a) $2 \times 2 \times 2 \times 2 \times 2 \times 2 = 64$
   b) $5 \times 5 \times 5 \times 5 = 625$
   c) $18 \times 18 \times 18 = 5832$
2. a) $3^4 \times 3^7 = 3^{(4+7)} = 3^{11}$
   b) $7^5 \div 7^2 = 7^{(5-2)} = 7^3$

c) $\frac{x^2 \times x^6}{x^3} = \frac{x^8}{x^3} = x^{8-3} = x^5$
3. a) $16^{\frac{3}{4}} = \left(16^{\frac{1}{4}}\right)^3 = \left(\sqrt[4]{16}\right)^3 = 2^3 = 8$
   b) $125^{\frac{2}{3}} = \left(125^{\frac{1}{3}}\right)^2 = 5^2 = 25$
   c) $25^{-\frac{3}{2}} = \frac{1}{25^{\frac{3}{2}}} = \frac{1}{\left(\sqrt{25}\right)^3} = \frac{1}{5^3} = \frac{1}{125}$

## Page 17
1. Rational:
   $\sqrt{16}$ because $\sqrt{16} = 4$ and $4 = \frac{4}{1}$
   $3 = \frac{3}{1}$
   5.03 because $5.03 = \frac{503}{100}$
   $\frac{8}{5}$, already a fraction
   $\frac{2}{3}$, already a fraction
   $0.\dot{7}5\dot{3}$, which equals $\frac{753}{999}$
   $0.\dot{4}$ because $0.\dot{4} = \frac{4}{9}$
   0.1283 because $0.1283 = \frac{1283}{10000}$
   Irrational:
   $\sqrt{3}$
   $2\sqrt{7}$ because $\sqrt{7}$ is irrational
   $\sqrt{12}$ because $\sqrt{12} = 2\sqrt{3}$ and $\sqrt{3}$ is irrational
   $\sqrt{32}$ because $\sqrt{32} = 4\sqrt{2}$ and $\sqrt{2}$ is irrational
2. a) $\sqrt{72} = \sqrt{36 \times 2} = \sqrt{36} \times \sqrt{2} = 6\sqrt{2}$
   b) $3 + \sqrt{5} - 2\sqrt{5} = 3 - \sqrt{5}$
   c) $\sqrt{27} = \sqrt{9 \times 3} = \sqrt{9} \times \sqrt{3} = 3\sqrt{3}$
   Then $3\sqrt{27} + 2\sqrt{3} = 9\sqrt{3} + 2\sqrt{3} = 11\sqrt{3}$
3. a) $\frac{3}{\sqrt{10}} \times \frac{\sqrt{10}}{\sqrt{10}} = \frac{3\sqrt{10}}{10}$
   b) $\sqrt{32} = \sqrt{16 \times 2} = 4\sqrt{2}$
   $\frac{4}{\sqrt{32}} = \frac{4}{4\sqrt{2}} = \frac{1}{\sqrt{2}}$ and $\frac{1}{\sqrt{2}} \times \frac{\sqrt{2}}{\sqrt{2}} = \frac{\sqrt{2}}{2}$
   c) $\frac{5}{2+\sqrt{3}} \times \frac{2-\sqrt{3}}{2-\sqrt{3}} = \frac{5(2-\sqrt{3})}{(2+\sqrt{3})(2-\sqrt{3})}$
   $= \frac{10 - 5\sqrt{3}}{4-3} = 10 - 5\sqrt{3}$

## Page 19
1. a) 805.9<u>97</u> → 806.00
   b) 45 578.92<u>027</u> → 45 578.92
   c) 12<u>4</u>3.304 → 1240
2. a) <u>1</u>273.097 → 1000
   b) <u>1</u>07.896 → 110
   c) 0.0078<u>06</u>4 → 0.00781
3. a) $1.34 \times 10^4$
   b) $9.06 \times 10^8$
   c) $3.238 \times 10^{-2}$
4. a) 1 306 000
   b) 9810
   c) 0.000 287

**5.** Accept any other variable in place of $x$:
   **a)** $97.5\,\text{m} \leqslant x < 98.5\,\text{m}$
   **b)** $1.5\,\text{mm} \leqslant x < 2.5\,\text{mm}$

**6.** $D = \frac{M}{V}$
   The upper bound of density is the largest mass divided by the smallest volume.
   Upper bound of $140\,\text{g} = 140.5\,\text{g}$
   Lower bound of $150\,\text{ml} = 149.5\,\text{ml}$
   $D = 140.5 \div 149.5 = 0.940\,\text{g/ml}$ (to 3 s.f.)

## Page 21

**1. a)** expression (as there is no equals sign)
   **b)**

| $s^2 + 3su - 4$ | Terms | Variables | Coefficients | Constants |
|---|---|---|---|---|
| | $s^2$ | $s$ | 1 (for $s^2$) | $-4$ |
| | $3su$ | $u$ | 3 (for $su$) | |
| | $-4$ | | | |

**2. a)** $3x + 5y - 5x + 3 = -2x + 5y + 3$
   **b)** $4j^2 + 3j - 1 + 2j - 4 = 4j^2 + 5j - 5$
   **c)** $5k - 7 + 3k - 9k + 1 = -k - 6$

**3. a)** $x = 2y + 4z - 1$
   $x = (2 \times -4) + (4 \times 5) - 1 = -8 + 20 - 1 = 11$
   **b)** $R = \frac{3x - 2t}{2}$
   $R = \frac{(3 \times 2) - (2 \times 1)}{2} = \frac{6 - 2}{2} = \frac{4}{2} = 2$

**4.** $15s + 25t$, where $s$ is the number of t-shirts and $t$ is the number of trousers.

## Page 23

**1.** $3(x - 3) - 2(x + 4) = 3x - 9 - 2x - 8 = x - 17$

**2. a)** $(x - 3)(2x + 5) = 2x^2 + 5x - 6x - 15$
   $= 2x^2 - x - 15$
   **b)** $(2x + 1)(3x - 5) = 6x^2 - 10x + 3x - 5$
   $= 6x^2 - 7x - 5$

**3.** $(3x - 1)(2x + 4) = 6x^2 + 12x - 2x - 4$
   $= 6x^2 + 10x - 4$
   $6x^2 + 10x - 4 - 5x + 8 = 6x^2 + 5x + 4$

**4.** $(m - 4)(m + 3) = m^2 + 3m - 4m - 12$
   $= m^2 - m - 12$
   Then $(m^2 - m - 12)(2m + 1)$
   $= 2m^3 + m^2 - 2m^2 - m - 24m - 12$
   $= 2m^3 - m^2 - 25m - 12$

## Page 25

**1. a)** $3(a + 3b)$   **b)** $5x(1 + 4y)$
**2. a)** $(x - 4)(x + 1)$   **b)** $(k - 2)(k + 3)$
**3. a)** $(2x + 3)(x + 1)$   **b)** $(2m + 1)(2m - 3)$
**4. a)** $(5y + 10)(5y - 10)$   **b)** $(4b + 9)(4b - 9)$

## Page 27

**1. a)** $C = 130 + 65h$, where $C$ is the total cost and $h$ is the number of hours worked.
   **b)** $C = 130 + (65 \times 4) = £390$

**2.** $T = P\left(1 + \frac{r}{100}\right)^n = 100\left(1 + \frac{4}{100}\right)^3 = £112.49$

**3. a)** $A = \left(\frac{a + b}{2}\right)h$
   $2A = h(a + b)$
   $\frac{2A}{h} = a + b$
   $\frac{2A}{h} - a = b$
   **b)** $\frac{2A}{h} - a = b$
   $\frac{2 \times 78}{6} - 11 = b$
   $b = 15\,\text{cm}$

## Page 29

**1.** Let $n$ be an integer. Then $n + 1$ and $n + 2$ are consecutive integers.
   $n + (n + 1) + (n + 2) = 3n + 3$
   $= 3(n + 1)$, which is a multiple of 3

**2.** Let $n$ and $m$ be integers.
   Then $2n$ and $2m$ are even numbers.
   $(2n + 1) \times (2m + 1) = 4mn + 2n + 2m + 1$
   $= 2(2mn + n + m) + 1$
   This is of the form $2k + 1$, which is an odd number.
   So by definition the product of two odd numbers is odd.

**3.** $a^2 - b^2 \equiv (a + b)(a - b)$
   $(a + b)(a - b) = a^2 + ab - ab - b^2 = a^2 - b^2$

**4.** $(x - 1)(x + 3) = x^2 + 3x - x - 3 = x^2 + 2x - 3$
   $(x + 1)^2 - 4 = (x + 1)(x + 1) - 4$
   $= x^2 + 2x + 1 - 4 = x^2 + 2x - 3$

**5.** 1 and 4 are square numbers.
   $1 + 4 = 5$, which is not a square number

## Page 31

**1.**

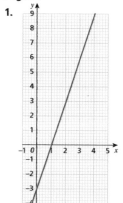

**2.** Two points are (0, 1) and (1, 4)

Gradient $= \dfrac{\text{Difference in } y \text{ values}}{\text{Difference in } x \text{ values}} = \dfrac{4-1}{1-0} = \dfrac{3}{1} = 3$

**3. a)** 3　　**b)** $-\dfrac{1}{3}$

**4. a)** Gradient = 2, $y$-intercept = (0, 5)

　　**b)** Gradient $= -\dfrac{4}{3}$, $y$-intercept = (0, 3)

**5.** Gradient $= \dfrac{5-3}{1-0} = \dfrac{2}{1} = 2$

　　$y = mx + c$

　　$3 = (2 \times 0) + c$

　　$3 = c$

　　Equation: $y = 2x + 3$

### Page 33

**1. a)** (0, 8)

　　**b)** (−2, 0) and (4, 0)

　　**c)** (1, 9)

**2. a)** (0, 5)

　　**b)** $0 = x^2 - 6x + 5$

　　　　$0 = (x - 5)(x - 1)$

　　　　$x - 5 = 0 \rightarrow x = 5$ and $x - 1 = 0 \rightarrow x = 1$

　　　　$x$-intercepts are (5, 0) and (1, 0)

　　**c)** $x^2 - 6x + 5 = 0$

　　　　$(x - 3)^2 + 5 - 9 = 0$

　　　　$(x - 3)^2 - 4 = 0$

　　　　Turning point is (3, −4)

　　**d)**

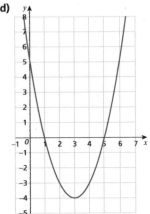

### Page 35

**1.**

| $x$ | −2 | −1 | 0 | 1 | 2 |
|---|---|---|---|---|---|
| $y$ | −7 | 0 | 1 | 2 | 9 |

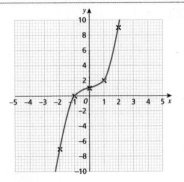

**2.**

| $x$ | −3 | −2 | −1 | 1 | 2 | 3 |
|---|---|---|---|---|---|---|
| $y$ | −1 | −1.5 | −3 | 3 | 1.5 | 1 |

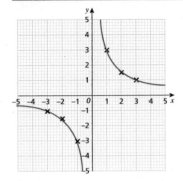

**3.**

| $x$ | −2 | −1 | 0 | 1 | 2 |
|---|---|---|---|---|---|
| $y$ | $\frac{1}{9} = 0.\dot{1}$ | $\frac{1}{3} = 0.\dot{3}$ | 1 | 3 | 9 |

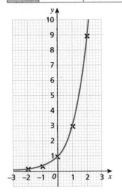

### Page 37

**1. a)** $g(3) = 3^2 = 9$

　　　　$fg(3) = (3 \times 9) - 1 = 26$

　　**b)** $f(2) = (3 \times 2) - 1 = 5$

　　　　$gf(2) = 5^2 = 25$

**2.** $f(x) = 3x - 1$
$y = 3x - 1$
$x = 3y - 1$
$x + 1 = 3y$
$\frac{x + 1}{3} = y$
$f^{-1}(x) = \frac{x + 1}{3}$

**3.** $y = 2(x - 1)^2$
$x = 2(y - 1)^2$
$\sqrt{\frac{x}{2}} + 1 = y$
$g^{-1}(x) = \sqrt{\frac{x}{2}} + 1$

**4. a)** 0.5      **b)** −1

**Page 39**

**1.**

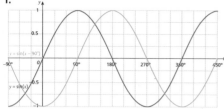

**2.**

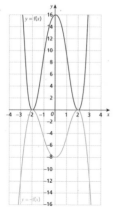

**3.** $y = \cos x$ is symmetrical about the $y$-axis, so a reflection in the $y$-axis does not change the graph.

**Page 41**

**1. a)** 10 minutes on his way to the shops + 25 minutes at the shops = 35 minutes

   **b)** The distance is the difference in the $y$ coordinates $(12 - 0 = 12)$ and the time is the difference in the $x$ coordinates $(90 - 70 = 20)$
20 minutes = $\frac{1}{3}$ of an hour
Speed = $\frac{\text{distance}}{\text{time}}$ = $12 \div \frac{1}{3}$ = $12 \times 3 = 36$ mph

**2. a)** 25 units     **b)** £1100

**3.**

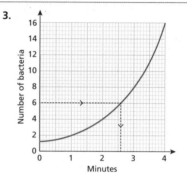

2.6 minutes

**Page 43**

**1.**

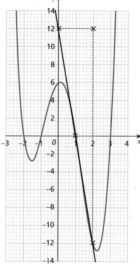

$m = \frac{-12 - 12}{2 - 0} = -\frac{24}{2} = -12$

**2.**

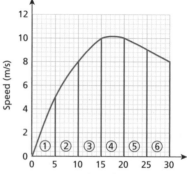

Triangle 1: $5 \times 5 \div 2 = 12.5$

Trapezium 2: $5 \times \frac{(5+8)}{2} = 32.5$

Trapezium 3: $5 \times \frac{(8+10)}{2} = 45$

Rectangle 4: $5 \times 10 = 50$

Trapezium 5: $5 \times \frac{(10+9)}{2} = 47.5$

Trapezium 6: $5 \times \frac{(9+8)}{2} = 42.5$

$12.5 + 32.5 + 45 + 50 + 47.5 + 42.5 = 230\,\text{m}$

## Page 45

**1. a)**

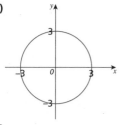

**b)**

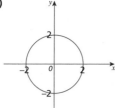

**c)**

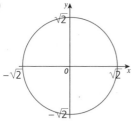

**2.**

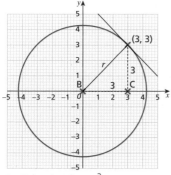

Gradient of radius $= \frac{3}{3} = 1$

Gradient of tangent $= -1$

$y = mx + c$

$3 = (-1 \times 3) + c$

$3 = -3 + c$

$c = 6$

$y = -x + 6$

## Page 47

**1. a)** $x = 4$    **b)** $x = 3$    **c)** $x = 4$    **d)** $x = -4$

**2. a)** $x = -3$    **b)** $x = 5$    **c)** $x = 5$    **d)** $x = 7$

## Page 49

**1. a)** $x = -3$ or $x = 8$    **b)** $x = 3$ or $x = -5$

    **c)** $x = -2$            **d)** $x = 2$ or $x = -3$

**2. a)** $x = 1$ or $x = 2$    **b)** $x = -\frac{3}{2}$ or $x = 4$

    **c)** $x = -\frac{1}{2}$ or $x = 2$   **d)** $x = \frac{2}{5}$ or $x = 1$

## Page 51

**1. a)** $x^2 - 5 = 4x \rightarrow x^2 - 4x - 5 = 0$

     $(x - 2)^2 - 4 - 5 = 0$

     $(x - 2)^2 - 9 = 0$

     $x - 2 = \pm 3$

     $x = 2 \pm 3 \rightarrow x = 5$ or $x = -1$

   **b)** $x^2 - 8x = 10 \rightarrow x^2 - 8x - 10 = 0$

     $(x - 4)^2 - 16 - 10 = 0$

     $(x - 4)^2 = 26$

     $x = 4 \pm \sqrt{26}$

   **c)** Rewrite as $x^2 - 12x + 26 = 0$

     $(x - 6)^2 + 26 - 36 = 0$

     $(x - 6)^2 - 10 = 0$

     $(x - 6)^2 = 10$

     $x = 6 \pm \sqrt{10}$

**2.** $3x^2 + 4x + 4 = 5$

   $3x^2 + 4x - 1 = 0$

   $x = \frac{-b \pm \sqrt{b^2 - 4ac}}{2a} = \frac{-4 \pm \sqrt{4^2 - (4 \times 3 \times -1)}}{2 \times 3}$

   $= \frac{-4 \pm \sqrt{28}}{6} = \frac{-4 \pm 2\sqrt{7}}{6} = \frac{-2 \pm \sqrt{7}}{3}$

   $x = 0.22$ or $x = -1.55$ (to 2 d.p.)

## Page 53

**1. a)** $x = -1$   $y = -5$    **b)** $x = 3$   $y = 1$

**2. a)**

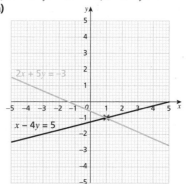

$x = 1$, $y = -1$ (accept answers within 0.2 of these values)

b)

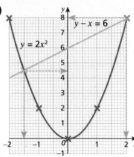

$x = -1.5$, $y = 4.5$ and $x = 2$, $y = 8$ (accept answers within 0.2 of these values)

## Page 55

1. a) $0 = x^2 - x - 5$
   $x^2 = x + 5$
   $x = \sqrt{x + 5}$
   b) $0 = x^3 - x^2 - 3x + 2$
   $x^3 = x^2 + 3x - 2$
   $x = \sqrt[3]{x^2 + 3x - 2}$

2. Let $x_0 = 1$
   $x_1 = \sqrt{1^2 + 5} = \sqrt{6} = 2.449$ to 3 d.p.
   $x_2 = 2.729$ to 3 d.p.
   $x_3 = 2.780$ to 3 d.p.
   $x_4 = 2.789$ to 3 d.p.
   $x^5 = 2.791$ to 3 d.p.
   $x^6 = 2.791$ to 3 d.p.

   The positive root is $x = 2.79$ to 2 d.p.

3. Let $x_0 = -2$
   $x_1 = \sqrt[3]{(-2)^2 + (3 \times -2) - 2} = -1.58740$ to 5 d.p.
   $x_2 = -1.6188$ to 4 d.p.
   $x_3 = -1.6180$ to 4 d.p.
   $x_4 = -1.6180$ to 4 d.p.

   The negative root is $x = -1.618$ to 3 d.p.

## Page 57

1. a) $2x + 1 + 8x + 5 + 2x - 6 = 180$
   $12x = 180$
   b) $x = 15$
   c) $2x + 1 = (2 \times 15) + 1 = 31°$
   $8x + 5 = (8 \times 15) + 5 = 125°$
   $2x - 6 = (2 \times 15) - 6 = 24°$

2. a) $A = (3x + 2)(2x + 2)$
   $= 6x^2 + 10x + 4$
   b) $6x^2 + 10x + 4 = 88$
   $6x^2 + 10x - 84 = 0$
   $2(3x^2 + 5x - 42) = 0$
   $x = \frac{-b \pm \sqrt{b^2 - 4ac}}{2a} = \frac{-5 \pm \sqrt{5^2 - (4 \times 3 \times -42)}}{(2 \times 3)}$
   $= \frac{-5 \pm \sqrt{25 + 504}}{6} = \frac{-5 \pm 23}{6} \Rightarrow$
   $x = \frac{-5 + 23}{6}$ or $x = \frac{-5 - 23}{6}$
   $x = \frac{18}{6} = 3$ or $x = -\frac{28}{6} = -\frac{14}{3}$
   c) When $x = 3$, $3x + 2 = (3 \times 3) + 2 = 11$ and
   $2x + 2 = (2 \times 3) + 2 = 8$
   When $x = -\frac{14}{3}$, $3x + 2 = (3 \times -\frac{14}{3}) + 2 = -12$
   and $2x + 2 = (2 \times -\frac{14}{3}) + 2 = -\frac{28}{3}$
   The dimensions cannot be negative, so $x = 3$
   So dimensions are 11 cm and 8 cm.

## Page 59

1. a)

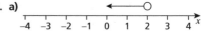

b)

c)

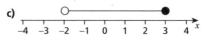

2. a) $x < 2$     b) $x \geqslant -1$

3. a)

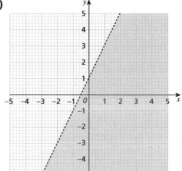

**b)**

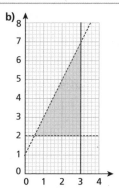

**Page 61**

1. **a)** 2, 7, 12, 17, **22**, **27**
   Term-to-term rule: Start at 2 and add 5
   **b)** 12, 8, 4, 0, **−4**, **−8**
   Term-to-term rule: Start at 12 and subtract 4

2. **a)** 1st term = 9          2nd term = 13
   3rd term = 17        10th term = 45
   **b)** 1st term = −3        2nd term = −8
   3rd term = −13      10th term = −48

3. **a)** $2n + 3$    **b)** $-3n + 20$

**Page 63**

1. **a)** 3, 6, 12, 24, **48**, **96**
   Common ratio: 2
   **b)** 81, 27, 9, 3, **1**, $\frac{1}{3}$
   Common ratio: $\frac{1}{3}$
   **c)** 1, −2, 4, −8, **16**, **−32**
   Common ratio = −2
   **d)** $3\sqrt{3}$, 9, $\mathbf{9\sqrt{3}}$, **27**, $27\sqrt{3}$
   Common ratio: $\sqrt{3}$

2. **a)** 4, 7, 12, 19, **28**, **39**
   **b)** 20, 10, 2, −4, **−8**, **−10**

3. **a)** 2, 8, **10**, **18**, 28    **b)** −2, −4, **−6**, **−10**, −16

**Page 65**

1. **a)** 5, 12, 21, 32, 45
   **b)** 4, 13, 26, 43, 64

2. Second difference is 2, so $an^2$ is $n^2$.
   Given sequence:   2   8   16   26   38
   $n^2$ sequence:      1   4    9    16   25
   Difference:             1   4    7    10   13
   The linear sequence is linked to the 3 times
   table, of the form $3n + c$.
   When $n = 1$, $(3 \times 1) + c = 1 \Rightarrow c = -2$, so the
   linear sequence is $3n - 2$.
   $n$th term rule of quadratic: $n^2 + 3n - 2$

3. Second difference is +4, so $an^2$ is $2n^2$.
   Given sequence: −2  −1   4   13   26
   $2n^2$ sequence:      2   8   18  32   50
   Difference:           −4  −9  −14 −19 −24
   The linear sequence is linked to the −5 times
   table, of the form $-5n + c$.
   When $n = 1$: $(-5 \times 1) + c = -4 \Rightarrow c = 1$
   $n$th term rule of quadratic: $2n^2 - 5n + 1$

4. Second difference is 8, so $an^2$ is $4n^2$.
   Given sequence:   4   15   34   61   96
   $4n^2$ sequence:      4   16   36   64  100
   Difference:           0   −1   −2   −3   −4
   The linear sequence is linked to the −1 times
   table, of the form $-n + c$.
   When $n = 1$: $(-1 \times 1) + c = 0 \Rightarrow c = 1$
   $n$th term rule of quadratic: $4n^2 - n + 1$

**Page 67**

1. $20.14 \times 10^2 = 2014 \, \text{mm}^2$

2. $6.45 \div 100^3 = 6.45 \times 10^{-6} \, \text{m}^3$

3. $16.5 \div 5.5 = 3$ so the scale factor is $\frac{1}{3}$
   $354 \times \left(\frac{1}{3}\right)^3 = 354 \div 27 = 13 \, \text{cm}^3$ (to the
   nearest $\text{cm}^3$)

4. For an enlargement with a ratio of $1 : n$, the
   ratio of the area is $1 : n^2$.
   $120 \div 30 = 4 \Rightarrow \sqrt{4} = 2$
   So the scale factor is 2.

**Page 69**

1. Use Pythagoras' theorem to find the length
   of the corresponding side in A.
   $\sqrt{6^2 + 8^2} = c^2$
   $c = 10$
   The scale factor is $10 \div 8 = \frac{5}{4}$, so the length
   of $x$ is $10 \times \frac{5}{4} = 12.5 \, \text{cm}$

2. **a)** Sides are 10 units and 6 units with the
   fireplace being 1 unit by 2 units. The actual
   distances are 5 m, 3 m and 0.5 × 1 m for
   the fireplace.
   The area is then 5 m × 3 m − (0.5 m × 1 m)
   = 14.5 m²
   **b)** A carpet that is 4 metres wide will cover the
   side that is 3 m, so a 5 m length is needed.
   4 m × 5 m = 20 m²
   20 × £13.99 = £279.80

**Page 71**

1. **a)** 1 : 4
   **b)** 2 : 5
   **c)** 2 cm : 100 000 cm $\Rightarrow$ 1 : 50 000

**d)** $15\,000\,g : 800\,g \Rightarrow 75 : 4$

**2. a)** Bottle A:
squash : water = 500 ml : 1500 ml $\Rightarrow \frac{1}{3} : 1$
Bottle B:
squash : water = 160 : 640 $\Rightarrow \frac{1}{4} : 1$

**b)** Bottle A requires a higher amount of squash per ml of water because $\frac{1}{3} > \frac{1}{4}$

**3. a)** $15 : 0.5 \Rightarrow 150 : 5 \Rightarrow 30 : 1$

**b)** $\frac{2}{5} = \frac{14}{35}$ and $\frac{4}{7} = \frac{20}{35}$

$\frac{14}{35} : \frac{20}{35}$
$= 14 : 20$
$= 7 : 10$

## Page 73

**1.** Charity X = £480    Charity Y = £720

**2. a)** Charity A = £18    Charity C = £36

**b)** £108

**3. a)** $\frac{4}{5}$    **b)** $120 \times \frac{4}{5} = 96$ adults

## Page 75

**1. a)** 150 g    **b)** 300 ml    **c)** 3 eggs    **d)** 75 ml

**2.** £0.90 ÷ 700 g = £0.001 286p per gram (to 4 s.f.)
£0.50 ÷ 500 g = £0.001p per gram
The 500 g bag is the better deal.

**3.** £4.50 ÷ 200 ml = £0.0225 per ml
£8.00 ÷ 500 ml = £0.016 per ml
The 500 ml bottle is the better deal.

## Page 77

**1.** 10% of 640 g = 64 g
30% of 640 g = 3 × 64 g = 192 g
1% of 640 g = 6.4 g
2% of 640 g = 2 × 6.4 = 12.8 g
32% of 640 = 192 + 12.8 = 204.8 g

**2.** 26.5 km = 26 500 m
$\frac{265}{26\,500} = \frac{1}{100} = 1\%$

**3.** £15 − £12 = £3
$\frac{3}{15} = \frac{1}{5} = 20\%$

**4.** £1200 × 1.03 = £1236

**5.** 20% increase so multiplier is 1.2
£3000 ÷ 1.2 = £2500

## Page 79

**1.** $y \propto x$
$y = kx$
$9 = 3x \Rightarrow k = 3$
$y = 3x$
$y = 3 \times 4 = 12$

**2.** $y \propto \sqrt{x}$
$y = k\sqrt{x}$

$16 = k\sqrt{4} \Rightarrow 16 = 2k \Rightarrow k = 8$
$y = 8\sqrt{x}$
$y = 8 \times \sqrt{25} \Rightarrow y = 8 \times 5 = 40$

**3.** $y \propto \frac{1}{x}$
$y = \frac{k}{x}$
$3 = \frac{k}{6} \Rightarrow k = 18$
$y = \frac{18}{x}$
$y = \frac{18}{4} = \frac{9}{2}$ or $4\frac{1}{2}$

**4.** $y \propto \frac{1}{x^2}$
$y = \frac{k}{x^2}$
$4 = \frac{k}{3^2} \Rightarrow k = 36$
$y = \frac{36}{x^2}$
$y = \frac{36}{2^2} = \frac{36}{4} = 9$

**5.** Ink used is inversely proportional to the number of pages printed.
At 600 pages a day, ink lasts for 3 weeks.
The number of pages printed has been divided by 3 (600 ÷ 3 = 200), so to find the number of weeks, multiply by 3.
At 200 pages a day, ink lasts for 3 × 3 = 9 weeks

## Page 81

**1.** Time = Distance ÷ Speed = 140 ÷ 40 = 3.5 hours

**2.** 11:05 to 13:15 is 2 hours and 10 minutes
$= 2\frac{1}{6}$ hours
Distance = Speed × Time = $2\frac{1}{6} \times 924 = 2002$ km

**3.** 11 kg = 11 000 g
Volume = Mass ÷ Density
11 000 g ÷ 19 g/cm³ = 579 cm³

**4.** Pressure = Force ÷ Area
60 N ÷ 0.012 m² = 5000 N/m²

**5.** Mass = Rate × Time
0.6 g/s × 180 s = 108 g

## Page 83

**1. a)** $S = 2000m$ where $S$ is the number of steps taken and $m$ is the number of miles walked.
**b)** $V = 500 − 50y$ where $V$ is the value of the phone and $y$ is the number of years.
**c)** $V = 12m$, where $V$ is the volume of water and $m$ is the number of minutes.

**2. a)** 7 miles

**b)** He drives faster from the coffee shop to work because the line is steeper than for the journey from home to the coffee shop.

**c)** Gradient = $\frac{\text{change in } y}{\text{change in } x} = \frac{20 - 7}{50 - 30}$
$= \frac{13}{20}$ miles per minute

$\frac{13}{20} \times 60 = 39$ mph

**Page 85**

1. $A = 1500 \times \left(1 + \frac{3}{100}\right)^5 = £1738.91$

2. a) $A = 25 \times 1.12^3 = 35$ foxes

   b) 3 years = 35 foxes
   4 years = 35 × 1.12 = 39 foxes
   5 years = 44 foxes
   6 years = 49 foxes
   7 years = 55 foxes
   After 7 years the population will have doubled.

3. $A = 1200 \times 0.84^4 = £597.45$

**Page 87**

1.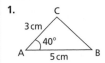

2.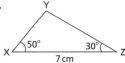

**Page 89**

1.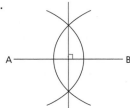

2.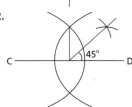

**Page 91**

1. a) $x = 120°$. They are allied angles.

   b) $y = 50°$. They are corresponding angles.

   c) $z = 70°$. It is vertically opposite the allied angle to 110°, or it is on a straight line with an angle corresponding to 110°.

2. The sum of the interior angles in a hexagon is
   $4 \times 180° = 720°$
   $90 + x + x + x - 7 + x + 12 + x - 25 = 720$

$5x + 70 = 720$
$5x = 650$
$x = 130$
The largest angle is $x + 12 = 142°$

3. Interior angle = 176° so exterior angle = 4°
   Exterior angle = 360 ÷ number of sides
   Number of sides = 360 ÷ exterior angle
   Number of sides = 360 ÷ 4 = 90 sides

**Page 93**

1. a) 180° − 38° = 142°
   (angles in a triangle sum to 180°)
   142° ÷ 2 = 71°
   (base angles of an isosceles triangle are equal)
   $a = 71°$ and $b = 71°$

   b) $d = 180° − 118° = 62°$
   (angles on a straight line sum to 180°)
   Angle $c = 180° − (90° + 62°) = 28°$
   (angles in a triangle sum to 180°)

   c) $e = 180° − 103° = 77°$
   (angles on a straight line sum to 180°)
   $f = 180° − (52° + 77°) = 51°$
   (angles in a triangle sum to 180°)

2. *Any one from:* kite; isosceles trapezium

3. a) $b = 75°$ (one pair of equal angles in a kite)
   360° − (2 × 75°) = 210°
   (angles in a quadrilateral sum to 360°)
   $a + 2a = 210°$
   $3a = 210°$, so $a = 70°$

   b) $e = 57°$ (base angles of an isosceles trapezium are equal)
   $c = 180° − 57° = 123°$ (allied angle with 57°)
   $d = 123°$ (allied with angle $e$)

**Page 95**

1. a) Yes, by ASA (or AAS).

   b) No, the side lengths that are equal are not corresponding sides.

   c) Yes, by SAS.

   d) Yes, by SSS.

2. Line AC is parallel to line DE.
   ∠ABD = ∠BDE (alternate angles)
   ∠CBE = ∠BED (alternate angles)
   ∠ABD + ∠DBE + ∠CBE = 180° (angles on a straight line)
   Hence, ∠BDE + ∠DBE + ∠BED = 180°, as required.

3. The reflex angle AOC is twice the size of $x$, as the angle at the centre is twice the angle at the circumference. Similarly, the obtuse angle AOC is twice the size of angle ADC.

Angles around a point sum to 360°,
so $2x + 2y = 360°$ giving $x + y = 180°$.

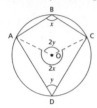

## Page 97

1. **a–c)**

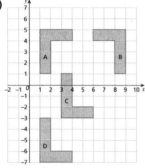

**d)** Reflection in the line $y = -1$

2.

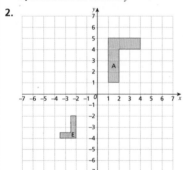

## Page 99

1. **a)** Cuboid

   **b)** Hexagonal prism

   **c)** Triangular-based pyramid/Tetrahedron

   **d)** Cone

2.

| | Shape | Faces | Edges | Vertices |
|---|---|---|---|---|
| **a)** | Cuboid | 6 | 12 | 8 |
| **b)** | Hexagonal prism | 8 | 18 | 12 |
| **c)** | Triangular-based pyramid | 4 | 6 | 4 |
| **d)** | Cone | 2 | 1 | 1 |

3.

## Page 101

1. **a)** $4.8 \times 100 = 480$ km (475–485 km is acceptable)

   **b)** $1.9 \times 100 = 190$ km (185–195 km is acceptable)

   **c)** $2 \times 100 = 200$ km (195–205 km is acceptable)

2. **a)** 318°–322°  **b)** 152°–156°  **c)** 026°–030°

## Page 103

1. **a)** Perimeter =
      $4 + 1 + 1 + 1 + 1 + 1 + 1 + 1 + 1 + 2$
      $= 14$ cm

   **b)** Perimeter =
      $4.3 + 3.1 + 1.2 + 1.7 + 1.9 + 1.7 + 1.2 + 3.1$
      $= 18.2$ m

2. **a)** Area $= \frac{1}{2} \times 4.2 \times 8.6 = 18.06$ mm²

   **b)** Area $= \frac{1}{2} \times (4.6 + 5.8) \times 1.9 = 9.88$ cm²

   **c)** Area $= 1.6 \times 3.2 = 5.12$ cm²

   **d)** Area of triangle $= \frac{1}{2} \times 14.9 \times 6 = 44.7$ m²
      Area of rectangle $= 30.2 \times 12 = 362.4$ m²
      Total area $= 407.1$ m²

## Page 105

1. **a)** $2 \times (5 \times 4) = 40$ cm² and $2 \times (5 \times 2) = 20$ cm²
      and $2 \times (4 \times 2) = 16$ cm²
      $40 + 20 + 16 = 76$ cm²

   **b)** Area of pentagon $= 27.5$ cm²
      Area of rectangle $= 4 \times 10 = 40$ cm²
      Total surface area $= (2 \times 27.5) + (5 \times 40)$
      $= 255$ cm²

2. **a)** Volume $= l \times w \times h = 5 \times 4 \times 2 = 40$ cm³

   **b)** Volume = area of cross-section × depth
      $= 27.5$ cm² × 10 cm = 275 cm³

3. Volume $= \frac{4}{3} \times \pi \times 6^3$
      $= 288\pi$ m³ or 904.8 m³

4. Volume $= \frac{1}{3} \times (5 \times 4) \times 9 = 60$ cm³

## Page 107

1. The corresponding angles are the same.
   $6 \div 3 = 2$ and $10 \div 5 = 2$ and $8 \div 4 = 2$
   The ratio of each corresponding side is 2, so the triangles are similar.

2. Triangle ABC is similar to triangle ADE with

side AC corresponding to side AE.
Side BC corresponds to side DE, so the scale
factor is $16 \div 10 = 1.6$
So side AE $= 8 \times 1.6 = 12.8\,\text{cm}$
Side CE $= 12.8 - 8 = 4.8\,\text{cm}$

**3.** For an enlargement with a ratio $1 : n$, the ratio
of the area is $1 : n^2$.
$400 \div 25 = 16$
$\sqrt{16} = 4$, so the linear scale factor is 4.

**4.** Scale factor $= 12 \div 4 = 3$
Volume $= 30 \times 3^3 = 810\,\text{cm}^3$

## Page 109

**1. a)** Diameter     **b)** Tangent
   **c)** Radius     **d)** Arc
   **e)** Sector     **f)** Chord

**2. a)** Circumference $= (3.2 \times 2) \times \pi = 20.1\,\text{cm}$
   (to 1 d.p.)
   Area $= \pi \times (3.2)^2 = 32.2\,\text{cm}^2$ (to 1 d.p.)

  **b)** Circumference $= 5.8 \times \pi = 18.2\,\text{m}$ (to 1 d.p.)
   Radius $= 5.8 \div 2 = 2.9\,\text{m}$
   Area $= \pi \times (2.9)^2 = 26.4\,\text{m}^2$ (to 1 d.p.)

**3. a)** Arc length $= \frac{\text{angle at centre}}{360°} \times$ circumference
   $= \frac{120}{360} \times 2 \times \pi \times 5 = 10.47\,\text{cm}$ (to 2 d.p.)

  **b)** Area of sector $= \frac{\text{angle at centre}}{360°} \times$ area of circle
   $= \frac{120}{360} \times \pi \times 5^2 = 26.18\,\text{cm}^2$ (to 2 d.p.)

## Page 111

**1.** Angle OYX and OZX $= 90°$ as OY and OZ are
radii.
Line segment YO $=$ line segment OZ as they
are radii of the same circle.
Triangle OYX and OZX share side OX as the
hypotenuse of both triangles.
So by RHS, triangle OYX is congruent to
triangle OZX.

**2. a)** $x = 32°$. Angles at the circumference, in
the same segment and subtended by the
same arc, are equal.
  **b)** $y = 56°$. The angle at the centre of the
circle is twice the angle at the
circumference that is subtended by the
same arc.
  **c)** $z = 88°$. Opposite angles in a cyclic
quadrilateral sum to 180° and there are
180° on a straight line (or by the alternate
segment theorem).
  **d)** $a = 65°$ by the alternate segment theorem.

## Page 113

**1. a)** $10^2 + 12^2 = x^2$

$x = \sqrt{10^2 + 12^2} = 15.62$ (to 2 d.p.)
**b)** $y^2 + 24^2 = 25^2$
$y = \sqrt{25^2 - 24^2} = 7$

**2.** Height of the triangle:
$a^2 + 8^2 = 17^2$
$a = \sqrt{17^2 - 8^2} = 15$
Area of the triangle: $A = \frac{1}{2}bh$
$A = \frac{1}{2} \times 16 \times 15 = 120\,\text{cm}^2$

The area of four triangles: $A = 4 \times 120 = 480\,\text{cm}^2$
The area of the square: $A = 16^2 = 256\,\text{cm}^2$
Total area $= 256 + 480 = 736\,\text{cm}^2$

**3.** Imagine cutting out a right-angled triangle
from the base of the cuboid.
$\sqrt{20^2 + 9^2} = c$
$c = \sqrt{481}$
Then imagine cutting out a right-angled
triangle using the diagonal of the base and
the side of the cuboid.
$(\sqrt{481})^2 + 12^2 = c^2$
$c = \sqrt{625} = 25$
The diagonal is 25 cm.
Alternatively, use $a^2 + b^2 + c^2 = d^2$
$d = \sqrt{9^2 + 12^2 + 20^2} = 25\,\text{cm}$

## Page 115

**1. a)** $\sin 42° = \frac{x}{10}$
   $x = 10 \times \sin 42° = 6.69\,\text{cm}$ (to 2 d.p.)
  **b)** $\tan 35° = \frac{8}{x}$
   $8 = \tan 35° \times x$
   $x = \frac{8}{\tan 35°} = 11.43\,\text{cm}$ (to 2 d.p.)
  **c)** $\cos x = \frac{4}{8}$
   $\cos^{-1}\left(\frac{1}{2}\right) = 60°$

**2.** Draw a right-angled triangle using A, F and C.
$\sin x = \frac{10}{15}$
$\sin^{-1}\left(\frac{10}{15}\right) = 41.8°$

## Page 117

**1. a)** $\frac{a}{\sin A} = \frac{b}{\sin B}$
   $\frac{12}{\sin 15°} = \frac{b}{\sin 25°}$
   $b = \sin 25° \times \frac{12}{\sin 15°} = 19.6\,\text{cm}$ (to 1 d.p.)
  **b)** $a^2 = b^2 + c^2 - 2bc \cos A$
   $y^2 = 5^2 + 8^2 - (2 \times 5 \times 8 \times \cos 120°)$
   $y^2 = 129$
   $y = \sqrt{129} = 11.4\,\text{cm}$ (to 1 d.p.)
  **c)** $\frac{\sin A}{a} = \frac{\sin B}{b}$
   $\frac{\sin 55°}{5} = \frac{\sin z°}{3}$
   $z = \sin^{-1}\left(3 \times \frac{\sin 55°}{5}\right)$
   $z = 29.4°$ (to 1 d.p.)

**2.** $A = \frac{1}{2}ab \sin C$

$\frac{1}{2} \times 8 \times 10 \times \sin 105°$

$= 38.6 \, m^2$ (to 1 d.p.)

## Page 119

**1.** $\begin{pmatrix} 5 \\ -3 \end{pmatrix}$ means to translate the point by 5 units in the $x$ direction and $-3$ units in the $y$ direction.

$1 + 5 = 6$ and $2 - 3 = -1$

Coordinates of B are $(6, -1)$.

**2.**

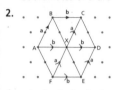

a) $\overrightarrow{ED} = \mathbf{a}$

b) $\overrightarrow{FC} = \mathbf{a} + \mathbf{a} = 2\mathbf{a}$

c) $\overrightarrow{FD} = \mathbf{a} + \mathbf{b}$

d) $\overrightarrow{XB} = -\mathbf{b} + \mathbf{a} = \mathbf{a} - \mathbf{b}$

**3.** a) $\overrightarrow{BA} = \overrightarrow{BO} + \overrightarrow{OA}$

$= -\mathbf{b} + \mathbf{a}$

$= \mathbf{a} - \mathbf{b}$

b) $\overrightarrow{AC} = \overrightarrow{AO} + \overrightarrow{OC}$

$= -\overrightarrow{OA} + \overrightarrow{OC}$

$= -\mathbf{a} + 2\mathbf{a} - 3\mathbf{b}$

$= \mathbf{a} - 3\mathbf{b}$

c) $\overrightarrow{CB} = \overrightarrow{CO} + \overrightarrow{OB}$

$= -\overrightarrow{OC} + \overrightarrow{OB}$

$= -(2\mathbf{a} - 3\mathbf{b}) + \mathbf{b}$

$= -2\mathbf{a} + 3\mathbf{b} + \mathbf{b}$

$= 4\mathbf{b} - 2\mathbf{a}$

## Page 121

**1.** a) *Any suitable answer, e.g.*

|  |  | Dice 1 |  |  |  |  |  |
|---|---|---|---|---|---|---|---|
|  |  | **1** | **2** | **3** | **4** | **5** | **6** |
| | **1** | 1 | 2 | 3 | 4 | 5 | 6 |
| | **2** | 2 | 4 | 6 | 8 | 10 | 12 |
| **Dice 2** | **3** | 3 | 6 | 9 | 12 | 15 | 18 |
| | **4** | 4 | 8 | 12 | 16 | 20 | 24 |
| | **5** | 5 | 10 | 15 | 20 | 25 | 30 |
| | **6** | 6 | 12 | 18 | 24 | 30 | 36 |

b) $\frac{3}{36}$ or $\frac{1}{12}$    c) $\frac{32}{36}$ or $\frac{8}{9}$

**2.** a) *Any suitable answer, e.g.*

|  |  | Spinner 1 |  |  |  |
|---|---|---|---|---|---|
|  |  | **1** | **2** | **3** | **4** |
| | **Red** | R, 1 | R, 2 | R, 3 | R, 4 |
| **Spinner 2** | **Red** | R, 1 | R, 2 | R, 3 | R, 4 |
| | **Yellow** | Y, 1 | Y, 2 | Y, 3 | Y, 4 |
| | **Blue** | B, 1 | B, 2 | B, 3 | B, 4 |

b) $P(R, 4) = \frac{2}{16} = \frac{1}{8}$ or

$P(R, 4) = P(R) \times P(4) = \frac{1}{2} \times \frac{1}{4} = \frac{1}{8}$

## Page 123

**1.** $\text{Relative frequency} = \frac{\text{Number of favourable outcomes}}{\text{Total number of trials}}$

$0.25 = \dfrac{15}{\text{Total number of trials}}$

Total number of trials $= 15 \div 0.25 = 60$

Relative frequency (Red) $= \frac{20}{60} = 0.33$ (to 2 d.p.)

Frequency (Green) $= 60 \times 0.3 = 18$

Frequency (Yellow) $= 60 - (15 + 20 + 18) = 7$

Relative frequency (Yellow) $= \frac{7}{60} = 0.12$ (to 2 d.p.)

| **Colour** | Blue | Red | Green | Yellow |
|---|---|---|---|---|
| **Frequency** | 15 | 20 | **18** | 7 |
| **Relative frequency** | 0.25 | **0.33** | 0.30 | **0.12** |

**2.** a) $\text{Relative frequency} = \frac{\text{Number of favourable outcomes}}{\text{Total number of trials}}$

$= \dfrac{26 \text{ red admirals}}{100 \text{ total butterflies}} = 0.26$

b) $0.26 \times 700 = 182$ red admirals

**3.** $P(3 \text{ or } 6) = \frac{2}{6} = \frac{1}{3}$

$P(2) = \frac{1}{6}$

Expected moves forward from 20 rolls $=$

$\frac{1}{3} \times 20 = \frac{20}{3}$

Expected moves back from 20 rolls $=$

$\frac{1}{6} \times 20 = \frac{20}{6}$

Total expected change from 20 rolls $=$

$\frac{20}{3} - \frac{20}{6} = \frac{40}{6} - \frac{20}{6} = \frac{20}{6} = 3.33$

A player can expect to move 3 spaces forward with 20 rolls.

## Page 125

**1.** a)

```
                              Yoga ── (30)
                    (80)
        Morning          Pilates ── (50)

        Evening          Yoga ── (60)
                    (100)
                         Pilates ── (40)
```

b) $P(\text{Pilates}) = \frac{90}{180} = \frac{1}{2}$

**2.**

**a)** $0.02 \times 0.02 = 0.0004$
**b)** $1 - 0.0004 = 0.9996$

### Page 127

**1. a)** $40 + 12 + 28 + 10 = 90$ students
**b)** 40
**c)** $28 + 12 = 40$ play rugby out of 90 total
So $P(\text{rugby}) = \frac{40}{90} = \frac{4}{9}$

**2. a)** Calculations:
$100 - 12 = 88$ take a tram and/or a bus
$35 + 68 = 103$
$103 - 88 = 15$ take a bus and a tram
$35 - 15 = 20$ take only tram
$68 - 15 = 53$ take only bus

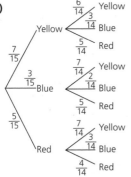

**b)** P(tram and bus) $= \frac{15}{100} = 15\%$

### Page 129

**1. a)**

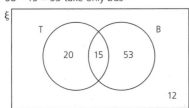

$P(Y, B) = \frac{7}{15} \times \frac{3}{14} = \frac{1}{10}$ and $P(B, Y) = \frac{3}{15} \times \frac{7}{14} = \frac{1}{10}$
$P(\text{one yellow and one blue}) = P(Y, B) + P(B, Y)$
$= \frac{1}{10} + \frac{1}{10} = \frac{2}{10}$ or $\frac{1}{5}$

**b)** $P(YR) + P(YY) + P(RY) + P(RR) =$
$\frac{35}{210} + \frac{42}{210} + \frac{35}{210} + \frac{20}{210} = \frac{132}{210}$ or $\frac{22}{35}$

---

**2.** 25 people work in sales, 10 of whom are full-time so $P(\text{full-time}|\text{sales}) = \frac{10}{25} = \frac{2}{5} = 0.4$

**3.** 5 people ordered all three toppings.
Chocolate sauce $= 20 + 5 + 2 + 23 = 50$
$P(\text{all three}|\text{chocolate sauce}) = \frac{5}{50} = 10\%$

### Page 131

**1. a)** Numerical (discrete)
**b)** Numerical (continuous)
**c)** Categorical
**d)** Numerical (continuous)

**2.** $\frac{12}{N} = \frac{2}{10}$ so $N = 60$
60 orcas in that region.

**3. a)**

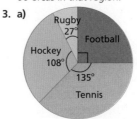

**b)** She is not correct. Although the proportion is greater, you don't know how many students are in class 11B so you cannot say whether there are more or fewer students who said football.

### Page 133

**1.**

| $x$ | $f$ | Cumulative frequency | $f \times x$ |
|---|---|---|---|
| 3 | 1 | 1 | $1 \times 3 = 3$ |
| 4 | 9 | $1 + 9 = 10$ | $9 \times 4 = 36$ |
| 5 | 6 | $10 + 6 = 16$ | $6 \times 5 = 30$ |
| 6 | 3 | $16 + 3 = 19$ | $3 \times 6 = 18$ |
| **Total** | **19** | | **87** |

**a)** Mode is the most common value, 4
**b)** Mean $= \frac{\text{sum of } f \times x}{\text{sum of } f} = \frac{87}{19} = 4.58$ (to 2 d.p.)
**c)** Median is the 10th value, 4
**d)** Lower quartile is the $\frac{19 + 1}{4} = 5$th value, 4
**e)** Upper quartile is the $\frac{3(19 + 1)}{4} = 15$th value, 5
**f)** Interquartile range $= 5 - 4 = 1$
**g)** Range $= 6 - 3 = 3$

**2. a)** $2 < x \leqslant 4$
**b)** Median is the $\frac{51 + 1}{2} = 26$th value, which is in the class $2 < x \leqslant 4$.

**c)**

| Class | Frequency, $f$ | Mid-class value, $x$ | $fx$ |
|---|---|---|---|
| $0 < x \leqslant 2$ | 10 | $\frac{0+2}{2} = 1$ | $10 \times 1 = 10$ |
| $2 < x \leqslant 4$ | 21 | $\frac{2+4}{2} = 3$ | $21 \times 3 = 63$ |
| $4 < x \leqslant 6$ | 13 | $\frac{4+6}{2} = 5$ | $13 \times 5 = 65$ |
| $6 < x \leqslant 8$ | 7 | $\frac{6+8}{2} = 7$ | $7 \times 7 = 49$ |
| **Total** | **51** | | **187** |

$$\text{Mean} = \frac{\text{sum of } f \times x}{\text{sum of } f} = \frac{187}{51} = 3.67 \text{ (to 2 d.p.)}$$

## Page 135

**1.**

| Age, $A$ (years) | Number of visitors | Class width | Frequency density |
|---|---|---|---|
| $0 < A \leqslant 10$ | 1480 | 10 | $1480 \div 10 = 148$ |
| $10 < A \leqslant 30$ | 2100 | 20 | $2100 \div 20 = 105$ |
| $30 < A \leqslant 50$ | 1620 | 20 | $1620 \div 20 = 81$ |
| $50 < A \leqslant 90$ | 800 | 40 | $800 \div 40 = 20$ |

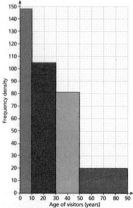

**Theme park visitors**

**2. a)** To find the median, draw a line from
$y = 3000$
Median = 25 years

**b)** To find lower quartile: $6000 \times \frac{1}{4} = 1500$,
draw a line from $y = 1500$
Lower quartile = 10 years
To find upper quartile: $6000 \times \frac{3}{4} = 4500$,
draw a line from $y = 4500$
Upper quartile = 41 years
Interquartile range = $41 - 10 = 31$ years

**c)** Draw a line from $x = 20$; there are 2500
visitors under the age of 20
$\frac{2500}{6000} = 42\%$ (to the nearest percent)

## Page 137

**1. a)**

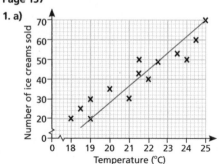

**b)** Draw a line from $x = 23°C$ to the line of
best fit and follow it to the $y$-axis.
53 ice creams (answers from 51 to 55 would
be acceptable)

**2.**

Ice cream sales per day

## Page 138–144

**1.** Perpendicular line has gradient $m = -\frac{1}{3}$ and
passes through the point $(0, 4)$.
$y = mx + c$
$4 = -\frac{1}{3} \times 0 + c$
$c = 4$
So the line is $y = -\frac{1}{3}x + 4$

**2. a)** $8(1 + 4x) - 4(x + 3) = 0$
$8 + 32x - 4x - 12 = 0$
$28x - 4 = 0$
$28x = 4$
$x = \frac{1}{7}$

**b)** $\frac{y}{2} - 5 = 11$
$y - 10 = 22$
$y = 32$

**c)** $2x^2 = 5x + 3$ can be rearranged to
$2x^2 - 5x - 3 = (2x + 1)(x - 3)$
$(2x + 1)(x - 3) = 0$
$2x + 1 = 0$ or $x - 3 = 0$, so $x = -\frac{1}{2}$ or $x = 3$

**3.** *Any two correct comparisons. One comparison must be the median and the other a measure of spread. You must state the values and compare.*
e.g. on average it's hotter in town B (median 23°C in B compared with median 11°C in A); the range of the temperatures in A is greater than in B (range for A is 40°C − 5°C = 35°C and range for B is 35°C − 10°C = 25°C); interquartile range for the temperatures in A is less than in B (interquartile range for A is 20°C − 7°C = 13°C and interquartile range for B is 30°C − 15°C = 15°C).

**4. a)** $8^{\frac{1}{3}} = \sqrt[3]{8} = 2$
**b)** $9^{-2} = \frac{1}{9^2} = \frac{1}{81}$
**c)** $125^{-\frac{2}{3}} = \frac{1}{125^{\frac{2}{3}}} = \frac{1}{\left(\sqrt[3]{125}\right)^2} = \frac{1}{25}$

**5. a)**

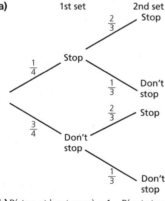

**b)** P(stop at least once) = 1 − P(not stop at both)
P(not stop at both) $= \frac{3}{4} \times \frac{1}{3} = \frac{1}{4}$
P(stop at least once) $= 1 - \frac{1}{4} = \frac{3}{4}$

**6. a)** and **b)**

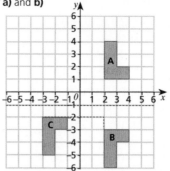

**7. a)** Liam has £$x$, then Kylie has £$\frac{x}{2}$ and Jack has £$(\frac{x}{2} + 5)$.
In total they have £20, so $x + \frac{x}{2} + \frac{x}{2} + 5 = 20$
**b)** $x + \frac{x}{2} + \frac{x}{2} + 5 = 20$
$2x + 5 = 20$
$2x = 15$
$x = 7.5$
Liam had £7.50 at the start.

**8.** Fridge World: £810 ÷ 3 = £270
£810 − £270 = £540
Fridge Bargains: 12 × £40 = £480, plus £100 deposit = £580
The Electric Store: £500 × 0.2 = £100
£500 + £100 = £600
Fridge World is the cheapest.

**9. a)** $I \propto \frac{1}{R} \Rightarrow I = \frac{k}{R}$
$10 = \frac{k}{24} \Rightarrow k = 240$
So, the equation is $I = \frac{240}{R}$
**b)** When $R$ doubles, $I$ will halve since $\frac{240}{2R} = \frac{I}{2}$

**10.** 7 + 5 = 12, then £84 ÷ 12 = £7
Abby gets two parts more than Jude and 2 × £7 = £14, so she is incorrect.

**11.** Angle ABD = 128° ÷ 2 = 64° because the angle at the circumference is half the angle at the centre.
Angle DBC = 180° − 64° = 116° because angles on a straight line add to 180°.
$x = \frac{180° - 116°}{2} = \frac{64°}{2} = 32°$ because angles in a triangle add to 180° and $x$ is a base angle of the isosceles triangle.
$x = 32°$

**12. a)** $(3 + \sqrt{5})^2 = (3 + \sqrt{5})(3 + \sqrt{5})$
$= 9 + 3\sqrt{5} + 3\sqrt{5} + 5$
$= 14 + 6\sqrt{5}$

**b)** $\frac{10}{\sqrt{2}} \times \frac{\sqrt{2}}{\sqrt{2}} = \frac{10\sqrt{2}}{2} = 5\sqrt{2}$

**13.** Volume of cylinder = $\pi \times 12^2 \times 30 =$
13571.68... cm³
Area of base of cuboid = $18 \times 16 = 288$ cm²
Volume of cuboid = area of base × height
So height of metal = volume ÷ area of base
Height of metal = 13571.68... ÷ 288 = 47.1...
= 47 cm (to the nearest cm)

**14.** The smallest angle is angle $A$
$\cos A = \frac{b^2 + c^2 - a^2}{2bc} = \frac{7^2 + 6^2 - 5^2}{2 \times 7 \times 6}$
Using the answer key on the calculator:
$\cos^{-1}(\text{ANS}) = 44°$ (to the nearest degree)

**15.a)** $6^2 + 5 = 36 + 5 = 41$

**b)** No, $n^2 + 5 = 125$
$n^2 = 120$ and 120 is not a square number,
or show $10^2 + 5 = 105$ and $11^2 + 5 = 126$

**16.a)** Area = length × width = $(2x + 3)(5x - 3) =$
$10x^2 + 9x - 9$
Area = 27, so $10x^2 + 9x - 9 = 27$
$10x^2 + 9x - 36 = 0$

**b)** $x = \frac{-b \pm \sqrt{b^2 - 4ac}}{2a}$
$x = \frac{-9 \pm \sqrt{9^2 - (4 \times 10 \times -36)}}{(2 \times 10)}$
$x = \frac{-9 \pm \sqrt{1521}}{20} = \frac{-9 \pm 39}{20}$
$x = \frac{9 + 39}{20} = 2.4$
Or $x = \frac{9 - 39}{20} = -\frac{3}{2}$ (or −1.5)

**c)** The longest side is $2x + 3$
$(2 \times 2.4) + 3 = 7.8$ cm

**17. a)**

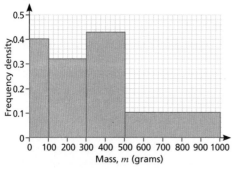

**b)** You would expect the proportion of
parcels weighing less than 100 g to be the
same. By the data in the table, 40 out of
240 parcels weighed less than 100 g.

$\frac{40}{240} = \frac{1}{6}$
$\frac{1}{6} \times 500 = 83$ parcels (rounded to the
nearest integer)

**18.** Angle $x$ combined with the angle of 34°
makes an alternate angle with the angle
given as 47°.
$x + 34° = 47°$
$x = 47° - 34° = 13°$

Angle $y$ is allied (or co-interior) to 34°
$y = 180° - 34° = 146°$

**19.**

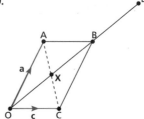

**a)** X is the midpoint of $\overrightarrow{AC}$, so $\overrightarrow{OX} = \frac{1}{2}(\mathbf{a} + \mathbf{c})$

**b)** OX : XD = 1 : 2, then $\overrightarrow{OD}$ is $3 \times \overrightarrow{OX}$
$3 \times \frac{1}{2}(\mathbf{a} + \mathbf{c}) = \frac{3}{2}(\mathbf{a} + \mathbf{c})$

**c)** $\overrightarrow{OB} = (\mathbf{a} + \mathbf{c})$, which is a scalar multiple of
$\overrightarrow{OX}$, so point B is on the line OD.

**20.a)** Factorising $y = x^2 + 6x + 5 = (x + 5)(x + 1)$
$x = -5$ and $x = -1$

**b)** Completing the square:
$y = x^2 + 6x + 5 = (x + 3)^2 - 9 + 5$
$= (x + 3)^2 - 4$
The turning point is at $(-3, -4)$.

**c)**

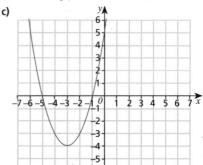